FENG SHUI
REVEALED

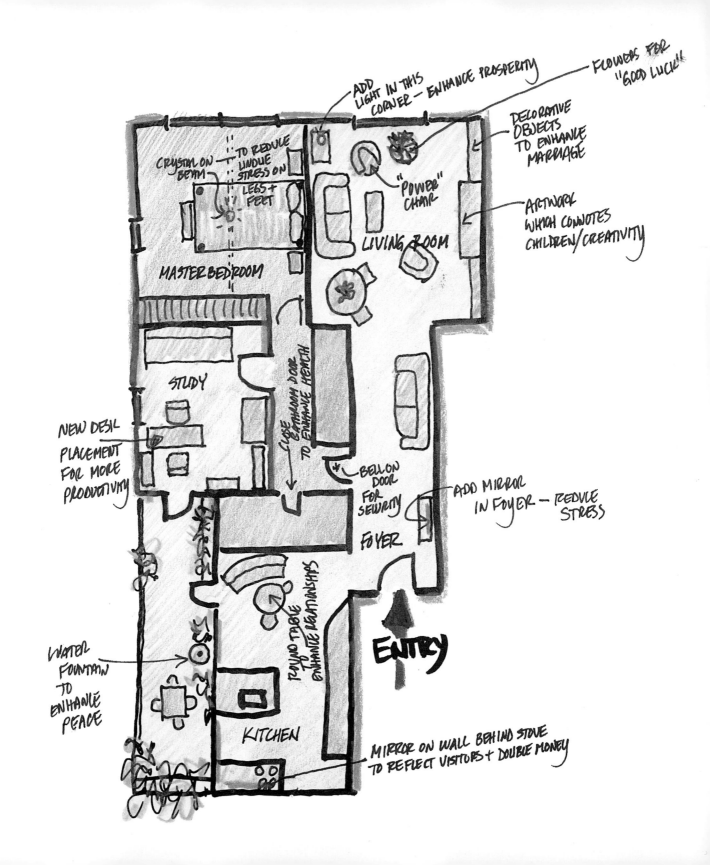

FENG SHUI
REVEALED

AN AESTHETIC, PRACTICAL APPROACH TO
THE ANCIENT ART OF SPACE ALIGNMENT

R. D. CHIN
WITH GERALD WARFIELD

PHOTOGRAPHS BY FRANCIS HAMMOND

Clarkson Potter/Publishers
New York

This book is dedicated to my parents, Eveline Moy and Thomas Wing Fu
Chin, with love, and to the lineage of the "Chin" family.

Published by Clarkson N. Potter, Inc., 201 East 50th Street, New York,
New York 10022. Member of the Crown Publishing Group.

Random House, Inc. New York, Toronto, London, Sydney, Auckland
www.randomhouse.com

CLARKSON N. POTTER, POTTER, and colophon are registered
trademarks of Random House, Inc.

Printed in China

Design by Lisa Sloane

Library of Congress Cataloging-in-Publication Data
    Chin, R. D.
    Feng shui revealed / R. D. Chin with Gerald Warfield; photographs by
Francis Hammond.–1st ed.   Includes index.
1. Feng-shui.   I. Warfield, Gerald.   II. Title.
BF1779.F4C4638   1998
133.3'337–dc21   97–20867

ISBN 0-609-60294-2

10   9   8   7   6   5   4

A C K N O W L E D G M E N T S

According to Chinese tradition it is appropriate to acknowledge one's beginnings. It was Sarah Rossbach's excellent book on feng shui that initially brought me to study under Professor Lin Yun; I am greatly indebted for his teachings, wisdom, and compassion. I am also pleased to number among my associates accomplished feng shui practitioners and scholars, including Professor Wang Yu de, Wuhan University, China; Raymond Lo, Hong Kong; and architect Howard Choy, Australia. All have contributed their expertise and time in reviewing portions of this book.

I wish to express special thanks and gratitude to the people whose houses appear in these pages. Their patience and generosity in allowing me and my team into their homes and in sharing their stories have been invaluable. I am indebted to them as well as to many others whose homes are not pictured.

A dedicated and talented support group saw this book through from proposal to completion: my agents, Ling Lucas and Ed Vesneske, who diligently and compassionately helped me progress along the difficult path in bringing forth this book; my committed editor, Carol Southern, with whom it was truly a pleasure to work. Her discerning perspective kept us all on track. Thanks to Francis Hammond for being the "right" photographer, and for his generosity in finding locations and his sensitivity and awareness in creating the picture-perfect feng shui shots; his superb assistant, Jont Enroth; Gerald Warfield, who carefully researched and crafted the introductory material and ingeniously wrote the distinctive stories from all

The photography team: Francis, Christine, the author, and Jont.

Gerald, coauthor

those endless nights of discussions and rewrites; Christine Churchill, who gave me a unique perspective for the Feng Shui Cures chapter as well as the appealing and sensitive styling of the locations; Lisa Sloane for the beautiful layout; Maggie Hinders for keeping the project on track through production; Mark McCauslin, Joy Sikorski, Steve Magnuson, and all the others at Clarkson Potter and Crown who extended themselves in helping to make my vision for this book a reality.

This project would not have crystallized without the help of many other dedicated and enthusiastic people: Tania Wremenko and Deborah Crowell, who with great patience and understanding helped me coordinate the logistics of writing this book while managing my office, and MaryAnn Myles, who transcribed tapes of the consultations. Of course, I would like to thank all of my family, friends, clients, and feng shui colleagues for their teachings and support and, especially, Nancy SantoPietro. Also, special thanks are due to the late Paul Rudolph, Nina Hughes, Scott Ageloff, Helen Weinstein, Eugenia Au Kim and Elya Horen, Sam Botero, Freddie Plimpton, Joanie Watkins, Catherine King, Jan Johnson, Rita Martins, Fred Charles, Keith Trumbo, Kerry Fidler, Steve Hanson, the New York Open Center, the Kushi Institute in Amsterdam, Jack Faxon, Marilee Talman, Iris Chiou, Ma Singfoon, Fred Nicholson, Rhoda Brooks, Martin Gonzales, the late Mitchell Lee, Anna Ulitsky, Stacey Griffin, Richard Schaublin, Peggy Troupin, Kay Lee, Jim Brandon and my constant companions, Boris the cat and Mozart, my miniature schnauzer.

I would also like to express appreciation to all those people and organizations that lent me supplementary art and furnishings for the photographs. To one and to all, I thank you.

CONTENTS

F O R E W O R D

Off East Thirty-sixth Street in New York City there is a little mews that few people know called Sniffen Court, a dead-end street paved with slate on which are perched ten tiny houses. Originally, they weren't houses at all, but stables for the horses of the grand folk who lived on Murray Hill. In the 1920s they were converted into residences. There is nothing special about them; architecturally they could be classified as Romanesque Revival, but otherwise they are undistinguished.

It is interesting to watch the people who pass this little enclave. Most are professionals, busy twentieth-century people whose faces reveal the stress of their everyday lives. But when they pass Sniffen Court something changes. Often they stop. Perhaps they smile. But for most only a faraway look reveals a moment in which tensions are forgotten . . . and then they charge on to the remainder of their day.

When we think about that scene it is remarkable. People stopping, peering longingly up an alley that dates from the last century. They are not viewing New York's great homes, but homes originally built as shelters for animals. The grooms and stable boys of the last century would have been astonished. Neither great wealth nor fine architecture is on display at Sniffen Court, nor does its appeal derive simply from its age. When we look at those little houses, something in our associations makes us feel good, and that *something* is absent from the majority of contemporary spaces.

It is my belief that with feng shui we can harness the power of these associations to create homes and workplaces that support us and give us a sense of well-being. It is also my belief that in the not-too-distant future we may expect designers and architects to concern themselves with feeling as well as with form and function.

The essence of feng shui is a harmonious relationship between you, the spaces within which you live, and the environment. This harmony and balance can be achieved by the application of a few fundamental principles, a healthy dose of common sense, and a willingness to listen to one of your own most trusted advisers: yourself.

I hope, in the pages that follow, to demonstrate creative and practical applications of feng shui to house and apartment interiors as well as to outdoor spaces. I hope also to reveal the mystical and divinational aspects of this ancient art both as a psychological tool and as an ingredient of architecture and interior design. An element of magic and mystery has always been associated with feng shui. Today, one of the distinctions between consulting a feng shui expert and an architect or interior designer is the personal issues that would seldom be considered within the context of design or architecture as those disciplines are practiced in the West.

Feng shui has the power to liberate a voice within us, a voice that needs to be heard, not only in our hearts but within the larger

I was fortunate in having the opportunity to work with one of the last master architects of our time, Paul Rudolph (below, on the right).

professional community as well. Those schooled in the West may still think of feng shui as so much smoke and incense, but the need is growing for another component within architecture and interior design, one that focuses on the individual and relates the objects within our spaces to our conscious and unconscious minds.

My discovery of feng shui was a revelation beyond anything my Western training had led me to expect. The deductive process, based on observations of nature, psychology, and immediate surroundings, pleased me. And since I had already come to the conclusion that the space of a particular person was truly a reflection of self, the focus on the individual felt right, as did, of course, the emphasis on associations and personal meaning.

I am a third-generation Chinese American. My early education and professional experience was as an architect and interior designer. Now I am also a feng shui *syan shang* or *gentleman* (as we were once called). This karmic combination of a Western education with an Eastern cultural heritage has placed me in a unique position.

There are at least nine major schools of feng shui practiced today. They differ from one another in the way they incorporate esoteric disciplines such as astrology, numerology, and phrenology, and by the manner in which they employ the ba-gua (the primary tool of feng shui). It is not my intention to ignore the contributions of any of these schools, and yet I believe that if feng shui is to have a major impact on the West, the focus must be in those areas that have credibility in scientific and professional circles.

The Chin family, Boston, circa 1921.
My father is on the far left.

The type of feng shui that I practice is derived from the teachings of Professor Thomas Lin Yun, whose work in this country draws on traditional Chinese philosophies and folklore, as well as on modern scientific method. Professor Lin Yun emphasizes a keen observation of the energy (ch'i) in both the individual and the environment, and, in the tradition of Black Sect Tantric Buddhism, he encourages the bringing together of knowledge from many different disciplines. In the use of the ba-gua I feel that Professor Lin Yun's reasoning is sound when he advocates its reorientation for each individual space—whether an entire piece of property, an apartment, or a single room—rather than working from a fixed direction for all sites, a concept that is distinctive to his practice.

My mentor, Professor Lin Yun.

In an ideal world, the intellect and the emotions would be of equal import; they would be in balance, as represented by the concept of yin and yang (the male and female principle). However, in my practice I usually encounter clients voicing their concerns intellectually. What I do is to invite more expression of the clients' feelings about their space to balance their reasoned approach. For me, feng shui is the music of space; it is a beautiful, dynamic, and healing art that, in the context of architecture and interior design, can be employed in the dual roles of reason and emotion.

 R. D. Chin
New York

PART ONE

INTRODUCING
FENG SHUI

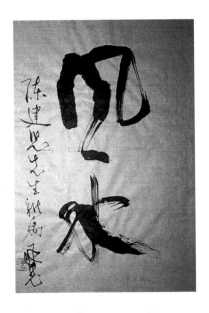

THE CONCEPT OF CH'I

The Chinese characters, cursive rendering, for wind (above) and water (below). Calligraphy by Ma Singfoon.

Feng shui, in its simplest form, is the practice of placing or arranging objects within a space so that they are pleasing to you and naturally support you within the context of that space. While architecture and interior design concern themselves with structure, function, and visual impact, feng shui takes into consideration the conscious and unconscious associations you may have with a space and the objects (and their placement) within it. These associations, of course, can be personal in the extreme, reflecting your most basic needs and desires. Feng shui accomplishes this by combining an ancient divinational tool called the ba-gua (explained in chapter 3) with simple psychology. An artful combination of the two is where the real work of the feng shui practitioner comes in. The result should be a house, an apartment, or even just a room that reflects your own values and aesthetics, that supports your personal ambitions, or that simply reminds you of your dreams. Indeed, with feng shui your castle should become your own in the most intimate detail, profoundly affecting the way you think about yourself and the world.

It is impossible to come to an understanding of feng shui without at least a basic awareness of ch'i (pronounced "chee"). In traditional Chinese thinking ch'i is the universal force or cosmic breath that all things are thought to possess. The character for ch'i 氣 is usually translated as energy, and there are, in fact, many similarities between the concept of ch'i and the assertion of modern physicists that all matter contains energy. However, unlike the energy of physics books, ch'i moves and flows much like water.

The Ming tombs were auspiciously sited, facing south with a mountain behind them.

The movement of ch'i is greatly affected by the area through which it flows. It can be slowed or deterred when encountering obstacles like trees, the sides of a mountain, or simply curves in a road. It can also be energized by moving objects, such as vehicular traffic or even people walking, and it can be accelerated by the inclination of a slope or sometimes by virtue of there being no obstacles, as in the case of a straight, unbending road.

Ch'i enters structures in a variety of ways. It can seep in through cracks or vents, it can rush in through large windows, and it can be generated *within* a room by electric lights, a fireplace, or even an argument. But the primary entrance of ch'i is through a doorway. Thus the main entrance of a room is known as the mouth of ch'i, and all objects within that room will relate to the flow of energy emanating from that source.

It was believed from earliest times in China that ch'i had the power to convey blessings from the dead to the living. Benevolent wishes of the deceased were carried from burial grounds (*Yin Zhai,* literally yin houses) to the residences of the living (*Yang Zhai,* literally yang houses). Though houses are yin in the context of outdoors, compared to graves they are yang. The location of grave sites was of major importance to families seeking the support of their ancestors. Grave complexes were usually located on nearby family land and carefully configured by feng shui masters so that the blessings were beamed toward the houses of current family members.

It is from manuscripts describing this process that we gain some of our earliest insights into ch'i. In a fourth-century scroll giving instructions for positioning graves we find not only one of the earliest references to ch'i, but possibly the first reference to feng shui. The words *feng shui* mean wind 風 and water 水 and it was through these elements that early geomancers sought to control ch'i. Feng shui, in its purest form, simply consists of ch'i management, which means keeping the energy moving, not too fast, and not too slow.

When ch'i moves too quickly, it invites natural disasters like precipitous slopes that threaten avalanches in the winter, or raging rivers that overflow their banks in the spring. One of the greatest achievements of the first emperor was the building of the Yellow River flood-control system. Equal in effort to the Great Wall, which he completed to the north, this system consisted of a series of dams, locks, and diversions of the river's course, segments of which are still in use today.

When ch'i moves too slowly, stagnation results. In quiet garden ponds fish were thought necessary to add motion lest the water sour and become a breeding place for mosquitoes. In the stories that follow you will see instances where ch'i is encouraged to slow down and collect, but never should it come to a complete stop.

The ch'i travels by the Wind,
And is stopped by the
Water's edge.
The old ones guide it
So it cannot disperse and
Move it so it cannot be still.
It is therefore named Wind
and Water.
—Guo Pu's *Rules for Burial*

When I refer to ch'i in nature, I have found that people seldom have any real appreciation of those forces. We are, today, so insulated by the marvelous products of engineering and technology that we are often out of touch with nature. Our ancestors, living closer to the earth, were sensitive to the ch'i even of a small hill because, for instance, they sensed the strain it caused the oxen or the horses that pulled their wagons. Today, in an automobile, we hardly take notice of a road's incline. Yet the forces of nature are still present and contain the same potential for good or for harm.

From earliest times mountains, hills, even gentle rises in the land were thought to possess their own energy, or ch'i. The higher the mountain the stronger the ch'i, and as the ch'i spread out from the highest point along the ridges of the lower peaks and hills, it decreased in strength. Using the analogy of the body, early geomancers saw in those patterns the "veins of the dragon": a force that wound its way through mountains and hills until it was finally stopped by water or dissipated onto flat land.

It was commonplace for feng shui gentlemen to recommend the placement of dwellings or cultivated fields on the south side of mountains (even low hills would do) so that the mountain's strength would deflect the northern winds, sparing crops the worst of early frosts and winter storms. Houses thus positioned were ideally situated to benefit from the gentle, warming ch'i of the southern sun. Assumed in the geomancer's recommendations was strict reverence for the veins of the dragon, which represented the strength of the

The Great Wall manifests the veins of the dragon.

Well-placed fields with mountains to the north.

mountain. Never could these veins be severed (such as cutting through a hill to make a road) without bringing bad luck and misfortune to the people who lived there.

To westerners this may seem little more than colorful folklore, fanciful association based on the profiles of undulating Chinese landscapes. Yet contained within this imagery is a concept that can be described in the objective terminology of science. For the veins of the dragon represent what physicists call potential energy, energy contained within a body that is not in motion, like water held back by a dam. Tons of earth and rock shoved high into the air by the movement of tectonic plates—which is what a mountain is—have stored within them incredible amounts of potential energy.

Long experience with landslides, avalanches, even erosion, taught the Chinese that cutting the veins of the dragon could release this force. Flat land, on the other hand, embodied no dragon and thus threatened no danger but it also offered no protection. It was seen as land exposed and vulnerable. In those feudal times, it was protection from malevolent forces about which the geomancers, and particularly their patrons, seemed most concerned.

Finding a site that came ready-made with a protective mountain to the north was not always easy. The Forbidden City, perhaps the quintessential feng shui structure, was built on a flat plain and so required the erection—at enormous effort—of an artificial mountain (now called Coal Hill) at its northern boundary to shelter the future abode of the Ming and Qing emperors.

Of course, the recommendations of the geomancers took aspects other than the topology of mountains into consideration. In the placement of villages such things as inclination and elevation, proximity to water, distance between houses, location of wood sources, and so forth were all examined in an extensive evaluation of the site. Sometimes dramatic catastrophes validated the geomancer's art. Rivers, for instance, offered object lessons to ancient peoples when raging floods overflowed one bank but not another. In the aftermath of such disasters patterns could be discerned in the deadly force, and feng shui practitioners learned from these experiences. In the floods that came to Hong Kong's Western New Territories in 1966 all the modern settlements were flooded, some even entirely swept away, while the traditional villages, positioned by feng shui practitioners, were left unharmed.

The Forbidden City; view from Coal Hill looking south.

It has been observed many times that feng shui contains generous helpings of common sense, but it also contains fanciful imagery. According to the Chinese, references to geological features are cloaked in images such as the black tortoise, the azure dragon, the white tiger, and the red phoenix. However, if we in the modern world are to benefit from the wisdom of the ancients, we must not be put off by this. We might even be inspired by it, and, when looking at mountains, or hills, or even at the curves of city skylines, see the sinuous coils of the dragon and feel the power that the ancients clearly recognized and that we ignore today at our own peril. ■

F U N D A M E N T A L S
O F   F E N G   S H U I

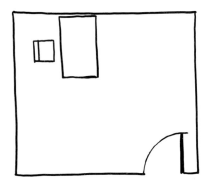

Good desk placement.

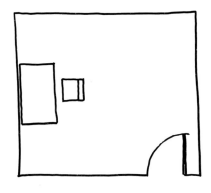

Bad desk placement.

The first practical application of feng shui I teach is that major pieces of furniture should be positioned in a room so that someone using them will face the room's entrance. Occupying such a position makes one feel much more comfortable and at ease. There are obvious psychological reasons why this is so.

Let us take, for example, the desk, one of the most commonly misplaced items in a house. Often it is positioned with its front to a wall or corner, partly because it monopolizes less space that way (which is true) and partly because it is thought that facing the wall will cut down on distractions (which is usually *not* true).

If, when sitting at your desk, you can see all the activities going on within a room, then you will feel much more in control of the space, and, surprisingly, this ability to see everything makes you *less* susceptible to distraction. If you are at a desk with your back to the main entrance, then, over a long period of time, you accumulate stress from the continual, even unconscious, thought that you must investigate what you hear but cannot see—or perhaps what you only imagine. This distraction can affect your focus and concentration on a day-to-day basis so that you may walk out of your apartment and forget your keys, or trip on the sidewalk because you are not completely aligned with yourself. Such things can happen because of something as simple as the location of your desk.

Psychologically, this makes perfect sense. We have an instinctive need to position ourselves where we will be safe, and we use all our senses to warn of danger. If you satisfy that inner need to be safe, then you maximize the chances for relaxation and rejuvenation. Sometimes clients assume that facing their desk into a corner or a wall will help them concentrate. As precedent they cite their college study carrels. However, the student at a carrel is not responsible for what transpires around him; the adult, on the other hand, is responsible for the home, and distractions that could be ignored in the library are to be checked.

Few principles, however, are without exception, and feng shui has a tradition that dictates that we always consider the entire picture—which sometimes changes everything. For this reason I try not to speak in terms of "bad feng shui," preferring instead to explain why certain configurations are powerful or weak and why they must be dealt with in ways that maintain balance within the space.

Another piece of furniture to consider carefully is the bed. In compliance with the first principle, it is always good to have the bed situated so that you are looking toward the door. However, it is thought to be bad luck to have the bed placed so that your feet point *directly* toward the door, as that is the position associated with dying: the position in which the body is carried from the room.

Of more importance is the space on either side of the bed. If a

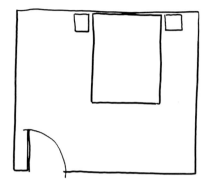

Good bed placement.

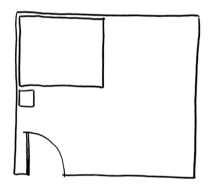

Bad bed placement.

couple sleeps in the bed, then an equal amount of space on both sides connotes equal standing of the partners. If one side is against the wall, it is a sign of a one-sided or unequal relationship because of the extra effort required to enter or leave the far side.

For the single person, a bed against the wall symbolizes that he or she may not be receptive to a relationship, a state which may or may not be true or which the person may or may not wish to change. For a child, a bed against the wall is beneficial in that it provides an added dimension of support. Likewise a slanted or overhanging eave can create a nurturing space for the young. A child's growing independence may be encouraged by a repositioning of the bed.

Another principle of feng shui is that a room's major features must be taken into consideration. Consider, for example, a hallway. The two longest walls are close together so that there is no place to go except forward. Thus the hallway's strongest feature is its forward motion ending in a wall or door. The door, as focus of the axis, is acceptable in that it invites us forward or at least promises that additional motion is possible. A wall, on the other hand, stops all movement, bringing the energy of the axis to a complete stop. This sudden interruption of motion creates a position of great strength that should be managed or softened, perhaps by the careful placement of objects of beauty or significance.

Depending on their size and position, overhead beams can have a powerful effect on the area immediately below. Since beams tend to divide spaces, this divisiveness, real or implied, can make one feel uncomfortable. Chinese folklore claims that sleeping under a beam creates problems, such as headaches and distress for the part of the body crossed by the beam. When clients complain that certain areas in their house do not seem right, I have been surprised at how often an overhead beam was the problem. Perhaps beams tend to be overlooked because they are out of the immediate line of sight and thus out of immediate consciousness. However, beams do have a long-term effect, and it has been my experience that one is more comfortable out from under them. If you cannot rearrange a room so that you do not spend a major amount of time beneath a beam, then you should mitigate the influence of the beam with a feng shui cure.

Central to feng shui is the concept of yin and yang. Yin is the female principle, rounded, dark, enclosed, nurturing, and soft. It is associated with rest, stillness, and even death. Yang is the male principle, characterized by light, hard surfaces, edges, and corners. It is expansive, aggressive, and associated with movement and life. The principles of yin and yang are universal and have nothing to do with an object being Chinese. Many notable architects and designers have carefully balanced these two elements in their works, intuitively if not consciously. In the stories that follow will be seen many examples of the balance or nonbalance of yin and yang. ■

Welcoming living room.

Unwelcoming living room.

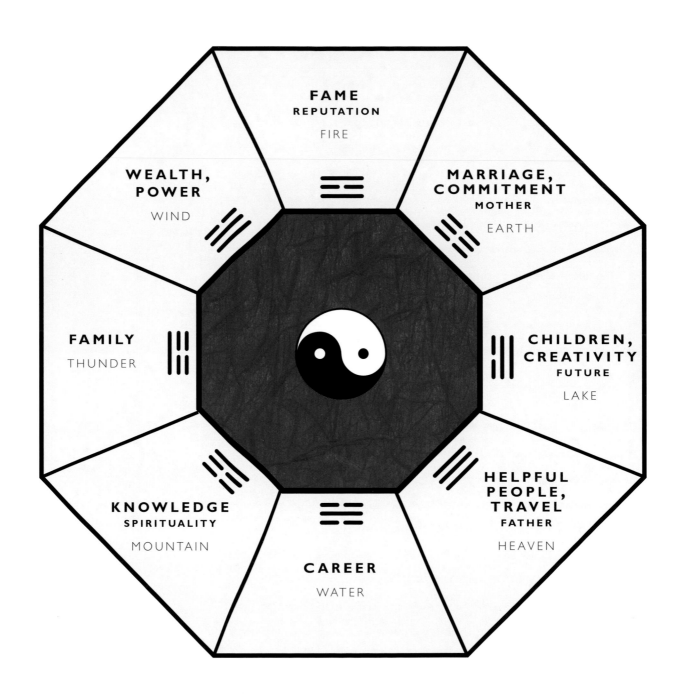

THE BA-GUA

3

THE   BA-GUA

The ba-gua is a feng shui tool used to analyze and evaluate a room, house, or tract of land. Once thought to be a magical talisman, it is simply an octagon with different trigrams (three-part figures) assigned to each side. *Ba* in Chinese means eight and *gua* means trigram, so the meaning is literally eight trigrams.

The trigrams themselves are made up of various combinations of two symbols, the male symbol ⎯⎯ and the female symbol ⎯ ⎯. Each trigram has its own attributes and those attributes are associated, by extension, with the specific sides of the octagon to which the trigrams are assigned. The trigrams, along with their meanings, can also be found in the *I Ching,* the classical Chinese oracle, although, in fact, the trigrams of the ba-gua predate the *I Ching* (as we know it today) by many centuries.

In the ba-gua you can see the attributes associated with each of its sides. They include fame, assigned to the top side, and marriage/ commitment immediately to the right. Continuing clockwise we have children/creativity, helpful people/travel, career, and so on all the way around the octagon. The middle position is associated with self and with balance.

The first step in a feng shui consultation is to superimpose this

OPPOSITE **The center of the ba-gua is the yin yang symbol—it represents the balance of all aspects of our life as represented in our space. The essence of feng shui is to bring harmony and balance within our inner selves as well as our exterior surroundings.**

octagonal shape on the floor plan of a room, or a house, or an apartment. The ba-gua will tell us the attributes that form the initial or rough perspective of that space. It is only after I have taken this step that I can begin to focus on the specifics of the space itself and on the client and his or her reasons for the consultation.

My approach, following the Black Sect Tantric Buddhist method of Professor Lin Yun, orients the ba-gua according to the entrance of the room, which is known as the mouth of ch'i. Thus, if we are standing in the main entryway, we are standing in the career wall, and the fame wall is directly across the room in front of us. It makes sense to orient interiors from this position, as it is without doubt the perspective from which most persons will view a room and form their initial impressions of the space.

For a specific example of how I use the ba-gua, let us take a square room with one door. If we orient the ba-gua to the door, we find that when we enter the space the top of the octagon represents the wall directly across from us. That wall becomes the fame wall. The corner on the far right becomes the marriage/relationship corner. The wall on the right becomes the children/creativity wall, and so forth, around the room.

When I speak of a wall or a corner as having attributes derived from the ba-gua, I am, in fact, referring not only to the wall or corner in question but also to the area of the room immediately in front of it. Thus one might have a couch or coffee table in the family area or in the wealth and power corner. In my own work, I find it useful to be flexible as to how far these areas extend. For instance, the wealth and power corner in the far left corner might stretch all the way to the center of the fame wall if there were some visual clue indicating that it was, in fact, being treated in that way. Such an inference could be made if a desk or a series of bookcases started in the wealth and power corner and continued halfway across the wall.

If there is more than one entrance to a room, then the main entrance or the one that is normally used first would serve as the mouth of ch'i. Equal use of two different entrances is usually avoided as, in traditional feng shui, it implies that the occupants of the space must of necessity travel a great deal. If the entrance is located on the far left or far right near either corner, it makes no difference as to the overall orientation of the ba-gua to the room. In many suburban and country houses, the back door is the door most frequently used. I do not consider this the main door; energetically, the front door still serves as the mouth of ch'i.

Before going deeper into specific applications of the ba-gua, let us briefly consider those attributes associated with the trigrams.

FAME. This is what you are known for or identified with, either personally or professionally. It might also represent your aspirations. *Fire is its element, its color is red.*

MARRIAGE/COMMITMENT. The personal relationship to which you are committed, such as to a spouse. It is also the mother corner, an area devoted to the maternal branch of the family or to nurturing or protection. Sometimes it is used for a future or desired relationship, or for professional commitments. (I have discovered that many of my clients are "married" to their work.)
The colors associated with this element are red, pink, or white.

CHILDREN/CREATIVITY. Current children or children yet to come, or even persons or things you consider to be your children, such as projects or creative endeavors. This is also the future area where you may indicate your aspirations or wishes.
The element is metal; the lake is the physical feature; the color is white.

HELPFUL PEOPLE/TRAVEL. The most yang of all trigrams, this is the area for strong people who may be helpful to you, whether friends, family, or business associates. The area of motion, it is interpreted as the place to celebrate your travels. It is the father corner and represents the paternal branch of the family.
The sky is the physical feature; the colors are white, gray, or black.

CAREER. Your professional life, usually your current profession.

Water is the element; the color is black.

KNOWLEDGE/SPIRITUALITY. Combining the intellect and the intu-ition, this is the mystical side of the individual. It is associated with the mountain, a place of meditation and enlightenment.

The mountain is the physical feature; the colors are black, blue, or green.

FAMILY. For current family—although it may be parents and ancestors as well—this wall may also be used for extended family or persons you consider to be family whether related or not.

Thunder is the element; the color is green.

WEALTH/POWER. This is the corner that represents the activity that supports you financially or sustains your influence or position. "Wealth," however, can be interpreted to mean things other than money or possessions, such as wealth in family or friends.

Wind is the element; the colors are blue, purple, or red.

BALANCE. The center of the octagon represent the self, and health. The yin-yang symbol represents perfect balance

The element is earth; the color is yellow.

The above attributes require care and subtlety in their interpretation. Often when applied to an actual site an area may not be literally what it seems. Due to a client's life, background, or associations with the space, wealth and power might be interpreted, for example, to mean the wealth that one possesses in a loving family. Or on the children's wall, one's creations, like books or paintings, might be considered one's offspring. Also, areas may overlap or intermingle with one another. For instance, symbols of one's career might be placed in the wealth and power corner instead of on the career wall to enhance the prospects of income. Diplomas might be placed on the fame wall as a marker or reminder of education or potential.

When I speak to clients about their space, we may begin by discussing general categories such as the above, but we can come quickly to personal issues relating to their innermost feelings. These are not areas that people necessarily speak about freely. In some cases it is helpful to keep a certain distance, and so I use the ba-gua metaphorically, or sometimes I use the terminology of architecture or interior design and speak, for example, about the bed location rather than a couple's relationship. When you read the stories that follow, keep in mind that often the references are metaphorical. I may sense a personal problem and recommend a solution without ever leaving the realm of interior design.

No discussion of the ba-gua would be complete without a mention of the geomancer's compass, called a luo pan (pronounced "low pan").

Also a tool associated with the practice of feng shui, the luo pan has an outer part that is made of wood and is about as large as a dinner plate, although the actual compass part, set in the center, may be only the size of a silver dollar. The luo pan is round, and bears multiple sets of rings, up to twenty-eight or more, to represent the various cycles and relationships thought to bear on a feng shui reading, such as the year, position of planets, and relationship of the basic elements. The innermost rings of the luo pan concern the earth, the middle rings man, and the outer rings heaven. A feng shui practitioner who uses a compass will be a member of one of the types of feng shui known generically as the compass school. Typically, this practitioner will also employ other esoteric disciplines, such as astrology and numerology, in conjunction with the luo pan to arrive at an analysis.

The ba-gua constitutes the innermost ring of the luo pan. When I give a consultation, I use only the ba-gua and do not refer to the outer circles. This identifies me as a member of the *form* school of feng shui as opposed to the *compass* school.

It was in the ninth century that a systematic approach to feng shui was compiled by a scholar named Yang Yun-sung based on observable phenomenon such as the natural formations of land. Yang lived in the province of Kuang-hsi, in southwest China, one of the most spectacularly scenic regions in the world. Its fantastically shaped hills and meandering rivers have been celebrated by Chinese painters and poets for centuries. He interpreted these natural elements as portents

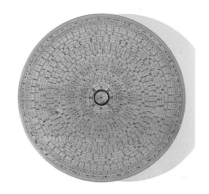

The geomancer's compass, or luo pan. Practitioners of the form school of feng shui make use of the innermost circle, known as the ba-gua.

Traditional luo pans made by the Wu family of the Anhui Province of China. LEFT Portable nineteenth-century model with sundial. RIGHT Contemporary model made from tiger bone wood.

that shaped the lives of the people who lived within this environment.

A hundred years later a scholar in northern China felt that the form school was too subjective and intuitive. As a result, a much more academic approach emerged that placed greater emphasis on the importance of precise mathematical calculations that took into account astronomical and calendrical formulas. This became the branch of feng shui known as the compass school.

While I respect the contribution of the compass school of feng shui, I have found that the structures and relationships embodied in the ba-gua are more than sufficient to produce a rich and rewarding reading, particularly in combination with the associations of the client. In addition, I feel that in using this, the oldest part of the luo pan, I am making use of the heart of feng shui.

Historically, the ba-gua did come first. The trigrams date from the earliest periods of China's prehistory and were already more than two thousand years old at the time of Confucius (b. 551 B.C.). The invention or discovery of the ba-gua is attributed to the mythical Prometheus-like emperor Fu Hsi, who was said to have taught his subjects to cook, to herd animals, and to farm about 4,900 years ago. Although our knowledge is scant, it is clear that the ba-gua predates by many centuries Confucius, Lao-tzu, and the Buddha, founders of the three major religions of China, each of whom made use of feng shui.

According to one legend, Fu Hsi first observed the ba-gua on the shell of a turtle. This is plausible, as the ancient Chinese practiced a form of divination called plastromancy, which read the future from patterns in the undershell of a turtle. Even today it is easy to see a similarity between the trigrams and the markings on the scutes or plates that make up the carapace of a turtle. Later, priests began using the bones of sacrificial animals. These bones, particularly the broad shoulder bones or scapulae, were heated; water was dropped on them and the resulting fractures were read. Large caches of scapulae have been found in ancient tombs, bearing engraved divinations.

It is amazing to think that we are still using this magician's tool in a modern world where atoms are routinely split and interplanetary travel is a reality. In an attempt to make feng shui more popular at the dawn of the twenty-first century, some have de-emphasized the role of magic and superstition. Yet at the heart of feng shui there is, without doubt, something left over from a time when animal bones were roasted over sacrificial fires, the future read in the patterns of their fractures.

Magic speaks to us as if from another realm where it is impervious to logic and safe from the scrutiny of scientific method. Magic has direct access to our subconscious; its appeal is immediate, and its terms are universal. Rather than ignore magic, I propose that we use it, that we listen to our inner voice, allowing it to express our deepest instincts. Though we may reject that voice by the power of our logic or our moral convictions, we should still listen, if for no other reason than that the voice comes from within us. ∎

PART TWO

FENG SHUI CONSULTATIONS

4

S P I R I T   O F   F A M I L Y

Catherine came to me after her husband, Steven, lost his job with a major New York brokerage firm. One morning he suddenly found himself cleaning out his desk and by that afternoon he was home with Catherine and their two sons wondering how many mortgage payments they could squeeze out of his severence pay.

The next day Steven appropriated an old desk for his new base of operations and placed it in the living room. From there he would transact what business remained, but mostly he would look for a new job. That was three months ago.

When I entered the couple's living room, Steven's desk was the first thing I noticed. It could not have been in a worse position: it required Steve to sit with his back to the room and to the entranceway. Such a placement works against concentration in that any sound or disturbance requires one to turn in order to investigate, thus becoming even more of an intrusion. But in this case the misplacement had more serious implications: one's back is the classic posture of vulnerability, not an effective position, psychologically, for someone looking for a job. Steven needed a work space that would provide him with better support and build his confidence.

The desk was also in front of a tall casement window (the mid-

Poor placement. Steven's former desk location in front of the window offered a dismal view of an adjacent building. Blocked views signify obstacles or difficulties with long-range plans.

OPPOSITE **Despite the strong desk position in the wealth and power corner, the living room is dominated by the family, as represented by the couches and coffee table. A strong female figure stands guard, a reminder that family needs not be displaced by Steven's job search. The red carpets symbolize good fortune.**

dle of three) so that there was light and that most sought-after of New York commodities: a view. But when I walked to the window I saw that it was a dim view indeed. Not twenty feet away, grimy windows punctuated the dirty brick walls of an adjoining building. Was this a view of success? And although he was at the edge of the future area of the room, he was facing outward, away from it. In other words, his back was to the future, and before him were only obstacles.

As if that were not enough, his desk subjected him to yet one more peril. Behind him and to one side was a slanted wall. (See the drawing below.) In feng shui, slanted walls are harbingers of the unexpected, and it is prudent to control the energy they create whenever possible. This particular wall ended by actually jutting into the room several inches, thus creating what is called a knife edge. This configuration added great force to the energy coming from

A slanted wall (signifying unexpected events) directed negative energy toward Steven's former desk location. The solution: relocate the desk across the room to the wealth and power corner. The energy of the wall, amplified by the knife edge, will be softened by a plant and a birdcage.

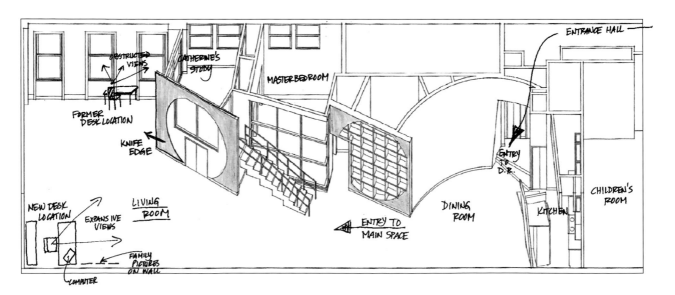

the slanted wall, which was, alas, aimed directly at Steven's back.

The placement of a desk should be considered carefully under any circumstances, even when the desk is largely symbolic (which it usually is when family members work outside the home). In Steven's case it was especially important that he be removed from the negative influences of the slanted wall, the blocked view, and the improper location. Ideally, his desk needed to be moved to an area of maximum strength and stability, and that meant the wealth and power corner. Fortunately, the wealth and power corner (always the far left corner when you enter a room) was unoccupied, and, in a lucky coincidence, it also turned out to be the wealth and power corner of the entire building. By that, I mean that as the condominium is a part of a larger structure, the building's feng shui brings its own energies to bear on the individual unit. When the wealth and power corner of a room or an apartment corresponds to that of the entire building (viewed from the main entry), then the location functions on two different levels, and the potential of the site is greatly enhanced.

To exploit fully the potential of the new site, Steven and Catherine purchased an executive desk with matching credenza. The new desk, now positioned in the wealth and power corner, was turned to offer a view of the family area and beyond to the dining room and kitchen, a view with both relevance and depth. The addition of a computer further energized the space, although the back of the computer, which faced the rest of the room, was an area of negative energy. (The backs of monitors, especially, need to be blocked,

Steven's desk is energized by its new placement In the wealth and power corner, and by a computer (an instrument of great energy) and a red mouse pad. Red is the color of highest energy (yang), symbolizing luck, success, and virtue. The plant absorbs negative energy from the back of the monitor and acts as a symbolic divider between work and family.

Taking its shape from traditional Chinese coinage, this money mirror offers a long-range view when Steven faces the wall. The plant symbolizes the nurturing of the family's wealth. The framed Japanese "fortune" foretold Steven's most successful year as a foreign currency trader, a year Steven would like to repeat.

OPPOSITE Steven's new desk position offers a perspective of the family wall (right) hung with portraits of the children and of the kitchen, the heart of the home. The negative effect of the slanted wall has been softened by an inset, circular bookcase.

if only symbolically.) For this a plant offered a temporary solution. The credenza was placed behind the desk and against the wall. Since a cramped space constricts the flow of money, the couple were careful to leave adequate clearance, a minimum of thirty-six inches, between the desk and its companion piece.

Steven's professional expertise is foreign exchange, so an appropriate object to hang above the credenza was a round money mirror. I call it a money mirror because its shape echoes the round coin with a square hole that has been the traditional form of Chinese copper coins since they were initially minted by the first emperor more than two thousand years ago. The round frame, which was painted green (a color associated with money in modern times), offset nicely the square mirror, which provided perspective from behind whenever Steven worked facing the wall.

The word *credenza* means "trust" in Old Latin, deriving from the fact that the sideboard was where the servants first tasted food before bringing it to the table. For the surface of this piece I suggested only objects of great significance. A plant was appropriate because watering it would symbolize the nurturing of the family's remaining assets. Steven also framed a Japanese "fortune," a souvenir from a temple in Tokyo that accurately predicted a year of record earnings in his former position. Also left on the surface was a red envelope from the blessing ceremony, which contained Steven's wishes for a new job.

After so much concentration of energy in the wealth and power

corner of the living room, there was a danger that the family would be overshadowed in what was, after all, a family space. According to the ba-gua, the family area within the room was along the wall directly in front of the desk. There the couple had already fortuitously placed living room furniture: couches, a coffee table, chairs, lamps, and so forth. In the new plan the furniture was pulled out from the wall and placed squarely in the middle of the room on an island created by another red carpet. This way the family, which was, after all, the reason for the job search, clearly dominated the room and reflected Steven's priorities.

One more balancing act was necessary in this space. The weight given the wealth and power corner needed to be further offset in the opposite (right) corner, which was the marriage/relation-

Balancing both yin and yang, the living room is expansive (yang) while Catherine's study at the top of the stairs is softly enveloped by curtains, making it a nurturing, yin space (yin). The problem: she sits with her back to the door. The cure could be the placement of a mirror or the hanging of a wind chime at the door.

ship corner. Coincidentally, Catherine had in her possession an object of major significance for her and her family: a beautiful female bust, handed down for four generations on her mother's side. This piece was strong because it embodied four generations of family maternal energies, and doubly appropriate because the marriage/ relationship corner is also noted as the mother representation. A heavy piece, it was capable of holding its own against the desk in the wealth and power corner.

But what of the slanted wall, which was also in the living room? I recommended nine plants to be positioned at the knife edge. Plants

The painting above the bed, mounted in an antiqued gold frame, signifies tradition. Two lamps symbolize the relationship, and equal space on each side of the bed connotes equal agreement between the partners. The area is warmed by a wool rose-pattern rug.

Resting beneath the bedroom lamp, a red envelope from the blessing ceremony holds Catherine and Steven's wishes, written on small pieces of paper. Two cranes on the envelope symbolize companionship and longevity. The envelope also contains rice, symbolizing abundance and prosperity.

are extremely useful in absorbing negative energy, and I proposed nine because in feng shui it is the most powerful of all numbers. It is the most yang, the most masculine (even its multiples), and it is the last of the single-digit characters in Chinese as well as Arabic numbers. Catherine felt, however, that nine plants were too much to care for and so we agreed to one. Realizing, however, that much of the negative energy might not be absorbed, we also decided that nothing should be placed in front of the window, the focus of the knife edge, where the desk formerly sat. Two other strong pieces were added near the knife edge to distract the eye from it and to enliven the dead area between it and the outer wall: a campaign chair (dark wood against the light walls) and a cage with two lovebirds.

Given the expansive, yang feeling of the living room, the rest of the condominium was appropriately more yin in nature. Both Catherine's study and their bedroom were excellent examples, unmistakably linked, visually, by the use of the same pleated sheer white draperies. These curtains established the feeling of softness and retreat from the rest of the apartment, giving a nurturing, almost womblike quality to both these rooms.

Catherine and Steven's consultation included a blessing ceremony. I asked both to write down their wishes, on separate pieces of paper, relevant to the areas of the ba-gua (wealth and power, fame, marriage, future, etc.), and these were read aloud at the appropriate points in the ceremony, and then sealed inside small red envelopes and left at each location. Because the children accompanied this tour

Curtains creating privacy and security shield sleepers from unexpected and negative events, as suggested by the angled railings.

of the space, the wishes for the bedroom (in the future area) that pertained to their marriage were not read aloud. In the photographs that accompany this story you will see the small red envelopes that were left from this occasion. Also contained in each envelope were a few grains of rice contributed by each member of the family. In the traditional blessing ceremony the feng shui master scatters rice around the periphery of every room. In this contemporary interpretation the rice was simply placed in the envelope along with the wishes. Rice is a symbol of plenty and prosperity, and in traditional folklore it also supplies food for the hungry ghost so that any spirit present in the house need not stir because of hunger.

In the center of the condominium the dining room was partially enclosed by a round wall on one side. The table located there is round, too. Since the time of the legendary King Arthur the round table in Western tradition has symbolized the meeting of equals. Here each member of the family could expect to have a voice.

In the kitchen, just beyond the dining room, the stove was against the wall, as is frequently the case in modern houses and apartments. This means that the cook must work with his or her back to the rest of the room, not the best position for the master of this space. Traditional wisdom has it that mirrors behind the stove "double the burners" and "double the food," thus increasing prosperity. But more important, mirrors as a backsplash are worth the effort it takes to keep them clean if they offer perspective into the rest of the room.

An altar in feng shui need not look like an altar nor make use of religious images, but a representation of the five Chinese traditional elements—earth, fire, metal, wood, and water—is necessary to symbolize the balance of all things in nature. At the main entrance to the condominium one is greeted by an angel, perhaps guarding the family, perhaps representing the spirit of the family. It was decided that this painting, attended by the five elements, would mark this console table as a sacred spot and set the tone for family and visitor alike upon entering the space.

An object of beauty on the fame wall sets the tone for guests upon entering a room. The painting of an angel protects the spirit of family, a common theme in this household. The space in front of the painting contains all five traditional elements.

Alexander, the oldest of the boys, placed the Quan Yin among his teddy bears. In the West, teddy bears represent affection and security. The Quan Yin, an Eastern icon, symbolizes compassion and protection of the weak.

OPPOSITE **The dining room table, located in the center of the apartment, symbolizes the family unit. Its round shape connotes equality. Mirrors lining the wall behind the stove are thought to increase the family's prosperity.**

ABOVE **The previous tenant, a man with AIDS, languished in this room for more than a year. Now it is the children's room, and we see that their spirit has overcome all negative feelings. Nothing of the former tragedy remains in this light and active space.**

RIGHT **Symbols of learning and nurturing dominate the children's room. Possible danger lurks in the angled railing of the fire escape outside (symbolizing unexpected events).**

I inquired about who had previously occupied the apartment and was told that the prior owner, a Dutchman with AIDS, had returned to Amsterdam to die in a hospice. Death is not categorically negative in feng shui. It can be synonymous with rebirth, transformation, and even the continuity of life. It is also thought that a space reflects the life of those who occupy it, so I could not ignore such a history. I inquired how the death of the owner affected the couple. Was he obviously sick? Were they depressed or frightened? To my surprise they said it was a tremendously positive experience. They had purchased the condominium when they first got married, before they had children, and they had agreed that the man could live on with them in the front bedroom. He stayed for a year before he had to be moved to a health care facility. They described him as a kind, sensitive man. Toward the end he became almost part of their family. It was after his departure that they were expecting their first child and converted his room into a children's bedroom.

As I spoke with them I realized that making this the children's room was not only appropriate but almost inevitable. The energy level of the children was capable of overcoming a great variety of influences, both positive and negative, just as, for example, they would be unaffected by the noise from the street outside. The children's room occupied the knowledge area, in the front of the building, also known as the mountain, which is the symbol of spirituality. Without consciously being aware of it, the couple had turned death into rebirth, into new beginnings, and into an affirmation of their own humanity.

Nine weeks after the consultation and blessing ceremony I heard again from Catherine. Steven had started a new financial company in New Jersey. They were both ecstatic. They would be moving to New Jersey, she said, to be closer to Steven's company. She asked if in their new home they should maintain the emphasis in the wealth and power corner. It was an interesting question. Wealth and power, I said, can be interpreted in many ways. It does not necessarily mean money or influence; it could be wealth the members of the family possess in one another and the power of their love and spirit. If Steven's new job remains secure I suggested that in the wealth and power corner of her next living room she celebrate her family, a wealth beyond all others. ■

Mirrors open opportunities, reduce stress, and bring more light into a space. To have no mirror or art here would present the walls as obstacles. Alexander, a quiet and studious boy, was promised the haircut of his choice if he passed the entrance examination of a private school in New Jersey. Here we see him thoughtful—with his new haircut.

5

F E N G   S H U I   D I V I D E N D S

Christine Churchill, formerly a magazine editor, is a consultant in the area of home furnishings and design. She and her husband, Keith Scott Morton, a photographer, have introduced feng shui into their terrace apartment at modest cost but with maximum results. Since the time of my initial consultation, the lives of both these creative people has dramatically changed. They sleep better in their apartment. They enjoy their terrace more. And even with all their new work, they feel a new tranquillity.

I prefer to begin a consultation by looking at an overall floor plan showing the relationship of the apartment to the building it is in. Using the ba-gua I saw that the apartment was in the marriage/relationship corner of the building, an area associated with nurturing and strong maternal instincts. This gave me the dominant aspect of the apartment, which I kept in mind, because often such an aspect will coincide with other issues that reveal themselves in the course of a consultation. Next I placed the ba-gua over the floor plan of the apartment, which told me the master bedroom was in the wealth and power corner, the living room in the marriage corner, and the foyer on the children's side.

A problem, which was clear from the floor plan, was that the

Blank walls connote obstruction and blockage. Here a framed mirror relieves the constricted feeling in the foyer and creates the possibility of more distant views.

OPPOSITE **Pulling energy from Central Park, which can be seen in the distance, this terrace succeeds because of the creative use of wood, water, and plants. All three combine to create a yin oasis that contrasts agreeably with the concrete and stone of the surrounding buildings.**

The round, yin shape of this table is a welcome relief from the aggressive, yang corners of the square table, now on the terrace. Switching the two was a simple, effective way to improve the breakfast nook.

apartment was missing a helpful people and travel corner, which should have been to the right of the foyer. A missing area usually requires some kind of compensation elsewhere within the space. The omission of this particular corner, also identified with the father, was corrected here in the foyer and also eventually addressed in the living room.

Starting from the front door, the foyer seemed somewhat bare. Blank walls, in traditional feng shui, connote blockage, incomplete projects, or thwarted plans. I suggested a mirror to remove the possible hint of barriers, to compensate for the missing corner as well as to bring into this space more natural light and energy from the adjacent breakfast nook. Chris selected a square, silver-leafed mirror, connoting earth and stability, and placed it above a side table. Mirrors, thoughtful and welcoming for guests, are almost always appropriate for foyers.

From the foyer we walked immediately to the left into the breakfast nook, just in front of the terrace door. Of necessity this area was small and made even smaller by the square dining table. When I placed the ba-gua in the kitchen space, I found the breakfast nook was located in the marriage/relationship corner where yin, round shapes are more appropriate than square. I therefore suggested switching the square table with the small round table on the terrace. The more yang, square marble table was perfectly at home in its new outdoor environment where there was more room to move around its corners.

The kitchen, designed by architect Claus Rademacher, takes

When using the stove, the cook has a view onto the terrace but only a side view of the kitchen. The best feng shui solution would have been to reverse the sink and stove so that the cook has a frontal view of the eating area.

The wok has been used for centuries to remedy line-of-sight problems in the kitchen. Of course, if it is in use it is not available for reflection, so Christine bought another for cooking.

maximum advantage of the northern exposure and every square inch of floor space. In feng shui terms the only negative was the position of the stove, because the cook had only a side view of the room. Again, the stove is particularly important because the future prosperity of the family is thought to be related to the preparation of food. That the cook should be unaware of his or her surroundings or vulnerable to surprise has unfortunate implications for the family. One solution of long standing is to hang a big, polished wok on the wall. The traditional thinking is that reflective surfaces near the stove double the burners and double the food. "When Claus and I chose the surfaces in the kitchen," Christine commented, "we actually discussed applying a sheet of reflective steel or aluminum behind the stove, but we never got around to it. This is perfect."

The next area we went to see was the terrace, situated in the knowledge and spirituality corner twelve stories above Madison Avenue. Plants and flowers visually softened the small sitting area, contrasting with the hard (yang) buildings surrounding it. I suggested a water fountain to add to the sense of a natural setting. When I returned some months later, I was pleased that the subtle sound of the fountain did indeed take the edge off sounds from the street

During a consultation, I make sketches to illustrate feng shui cures.

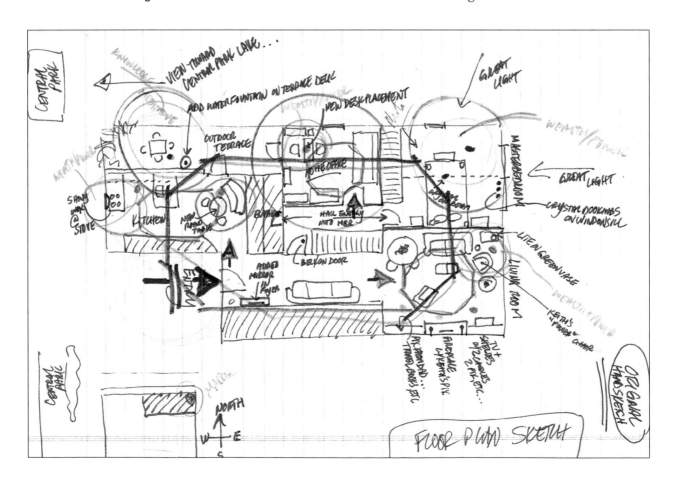

below. That, together with the strong presence of wood and abundant plants and flowers, seemed to shield this oasis in the middle of New York City. "Depending on the season," commented Christine, "we really experience our apartment differently. Spring and summer means the terrace is in bloom and we are drawn to that part of the house. When fall and winter come, the living room fireplace makes the living room the center."

The other room off the terrace was Chris's home office, which doubles as a guest room. Central to the changes here was pulling the narrow Parsons table, used as a desk, away from the wall. Now Chris has a choice of either side of the desk. "I found that I had been working less and less at my desk when it was facing the wall. I just didn't enjoy it—and consequently, papers ended up scattered all over the house." On either side of the table she would now face one door, but

By moving the desk out from the wall, Christine has a perspective no matter at which side she sits.

The door opens onto the right side of the bed, subjecting that side to the energy from the hallway and drafts from cross-ventilation. Christine slept better when Keith took the yang side, closer to the door.

she would have her back to the other. The more important door was the one from inside the apartment. For those times when she had her back to that door, we mounted a bell in the hallway so that someone coming toward her private space would be heard. This also served as correction for the incorrect bed placement in the master bedroom.

The bedroom was in many ways the most interesting room of the apartment. It is a very powerful room because it is positioned in the marriage/relationship corner for the entire building, a location that usually indicates good relationships. Relative to the front door of the apartment, it is in the wealth and power corner, which adds strength to the relationship. Unfortunately, however, the arrangement of doors, windows, and closets forced the queen-size bed into an incorrect position. I asked Christine how she slept, and she said that sleeping on the side closest to the door she could feel the cross-ventilation, which made her a little uncomfortable, but that Keith seemed to sleep very well. The solution was clear. Keith's yang nature could better accommodate the energy from the doorway while Chris needed more of a yin feeling of calm. The couple took my suggestion, switching sides, and the problem was solved without further corrections.

There was more, however, to this complicated room. Chris had designed the beautiful four-poster bed with its softly curving headboard promising a comforting sleep. I interpreted the four posters of the bed to represent the legendary four columns that hold up the canopy of heaven. But in this case heaven had something else in store in the form of a beam that crossed the foot of the bed.

The crystal chandelier hanging in the center of the room was too far away to correct the beam placement. I saw three choices: to add a canopy to the bed, to hang a single crystal from the beam, or to mount a bamboo flute at either end of the beam. Chris chose the crystal, as it was the most unobtrusive.

Crystals were abundantly at hand in the form of Chris's vintage doorknob collection, usually kept on the bedroom windowsill, where the individual crystals could spread their refracted light. These were some of Chris's favorite flea market acquisitions. She hung one on the overhead beam to fragment its energy. Traditionally,

A crystal deflects the energy of a ceiling beam that crosses the foot of the couple's bed.

Christine's collection of crystal doorknobs refract the morning sun, creating a healing rainbow of colors.

The wealth and power corner is enlivened by a Noguchi lamp, candles, reflective glass, and even an electric light inside the urn. Stimulating this important corner was necessary to create a balance of energy.

OPPOSITE The polished wood floor acts as a reflective surface, supplying the room with warmth from the sunlight. The tones are picked up in the delicate green of the walls and upholstery.

a crystal is hung with red cord or ribbon to mark the auspiciousness of the piece and to call attention to it. Perhaps this is because cut crystals tend to be small. Chris, however, felt that the color red was out of place with her decor and so decided on a tie of white organdy ribbon. I found no objection to this, as one of the objectives of feng shui is to create a harmonious environment, and Chris's solution was to do exactly that.

We entered the living room, located in the fame and relationship area. Fame can be interpreted as the first impression of how the occupants are perceived by family and friends. This room, decorated by Chris, reflects her taste and style. It was originally painted a creamy off-white, but Chris wanted to change it to a more active color, and asked me what would be appropriate from a feng shui perspective. I suggested a few colors such as rose for relationships, green for new growth, and yellow for sunshine energy. She selected a color she dubbed "young bamboo green," symbolizing the growth of new beginnings.

To enliven the wealth and power corner of the living room, I suggested a chair for Chris's husband. (Keith loved the idea of finding a chair for himself for this corner.) We further energized this area with candles and electric lights. Interestingly, an urn placed there already had a hole at its base, which we could wire for indirect lighting. I asked Chris about the large photograph of a young girl next to the urn. "This picture was taken while we were in Venice. I felt that it was yet another ode to Italian light and its amazing qualities."

The helpful people and travel corner is associated with strong, yang figures. The painting was given to Christine by her father.

TOP RIGHT A photograph, by Keith, of an oddly formed tree rests on the oak mantel in the future/creativity side of the living room. Wood is a symbol of growth and expansion.

RIGHT In the marriage/relationship corner Christine has placed two paintings of vessels (feminine symbols), two candlesticks (male symbols), and a photograph of a baby, symbolizing birth and renewal.

The fireplace is located on the right side of the living room. When I arrived, it was otherwise a blank wall; Chris and Keith had not decided what to place there. Since this is the children/creativity area, I thought that a piece of artwork the two of them chose together would be appropriate. Chris picked one of Keith's photographs, a topiary tree that had great meaning for her because she remembered Keith's playful mood as he was taking the shot. She said it truly reminded her of how he still expresses himself creatively—as if he was seeing the world for the first time.

The marriage/relationship corner of the living room was occupied by a TV. Chris asked how she could enhance this area, and I suggested items connoting a couple. She produced two paintings of vases by a close female friend that she said represented feminine energy. I proposed the addition of candlesticks to balance it with male energy. She also chose a picture of her nephew, which I interpreted as a reflection of the nurturing or maternal aspect associated with that area.

In the marriage/relationship corner Christine has placed a conscious and artful juxtaposition of symbolic objects. The two candlesticks, the two pictures of vessels, and a photograph of a baby rest on the shelf and speak quietly to the constancy of this couple and their creativity. ■

6

G E N T L E   R E M I N D E R S

Rosalina Leung is a young fashion designer. On a modest budget she has put together an apartment with a tasteful balance of collectibles and items of her own making. Her next step is to set up her own business. With confidence and quiet sensibility she spoke of feng shui and her future: "The feng shui helps me before going on to my next endeavor—it helps to position me comfortably in my own space."

When you enter Rosalina's apartment, you step first into an enclosed, nurturing foyer expanded somewhat by a welcoming mirror at eye level. A bowl of potpourri presented on a tripod pleases the senses and softens the narrow sliver of wall that marks the beginning of the hallway. A muslin curtain is gently drawn back as if to gradually reveal the apartment beyond.

It wasn't always that way. At the time of our consultation I observed the figure of a knife edge appearing on the lower part of the ceiling pointing directly to the entry door on the right side of the hall. This unfortunate effect has now been completely obscured by the curtain that Rosalina made only a few days later. Now we feel only the enticement of polished wooden floors and the warmth of the walls. Two plants offer a touch of green, creating alternatives to the strong focal points of the hall axes.

OPPOSITE **The curtain both obscures an offending knife edge and invites us into the rest of the apartment. Two plants create focal points and help absorb the strong ch'i directed down the hall.**

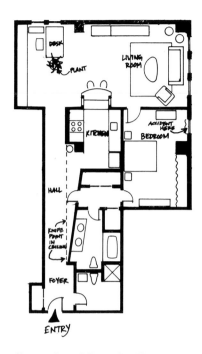

Cleaver-shaped floor plan. The right-hand wall is the cutting edge, which necessitates careful furniture placement along that wall.

More than halfway down the hall, the first plant, resting on a small stand, slows the motion of the ch'i and offers the very practical benefit of masking the building's intercom phone. It should also be noted that the wood of the hallway floor is laid crossways to its length. If it had been lengthwise, the forward motion of ch'i would have been much stronger and even more difficult to slow except, perhaps, with a rug.

At the end of the hall is the main living space and Rosalina's desk, in the wealth and power corner. However, too much energy still barrels down the hall and into the desk. True, she is launching a new business, and that is, right now, her primary focus, but a bare desk at the end of such a strong axis would lack Rosalina's characteristics of subtlety and tact. Although the effect on her would be perhaps only to disturb her concentration occasionally, it would be best to correct. We agreed, therefore, to place a plant at the end of the desk to absorb the energy. Plants are great absorbers of ch'i, and the care they require further reinforces their purpose in the minds of their owners.

Another problem in this deceivingly simple floor plan is a window above the desk, which is on the center axis point of the hall. Traditional thinking would maintain that when the window is open, the energy from the hall would continue its momentum, rushing right past Rosalina and through to the outdoors. One of the precepts of ch'i management is to control energy flow so that it lingers in areas where it is needed, providing a store of energy, but does not

Rosalina would receive full brunt of the energy from the hall if not protected by a small tree. At the upper left of the hallway ceiling you can see the cutout for the kitchen, which, from the entry, gives the impression of the point of a knife.

linger too long, lest it stagnate. In this way it is somewhat like a river. In a straight line a river can build too much forward momentum. Gentle curves preserve the right amount of energy while truly tortuous curves can block energy to the point of stagnation of overflow. The energy is slowed by keeping the blinds of the window closed, but it is not blocked because it is redirected into the rest of the apartment.

Behind Rosalina's desk, in a built-in cabinet unit that holds her computers, there is a place for an altar. Rosalina has placed here a ceramic Quan Yin, a female symbol of protection, a delicately carved vertical incense holder, and a small lacquer bowl of water. These spiritual reminders are a beneficial source of strength. Interestingly, this altar is located in the knowledge corner, which also connotes a place of meditation.

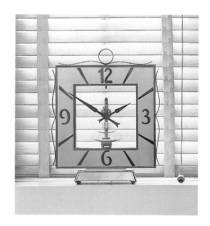

A heavy clock with a pendulum, a traditional cure, was recommended by another feng shui practitioner to stop ch'i from escaping through the window.

In the spirituality corner an altar holds a Quan Yin, a carved vertical incense holder, and a small lacquer bowl of purifying water.

RIGHT **Rosalina's desk in the wealth and power corner is backed by her extensive library. Her computer resides in the built-in cabinets. The smooth surface of the cabinet doors and inset altar contrast with the vitality of the book shelves to form a striking balance of yin and yang.**

OPPOSITE **From her desk Rosalina observes the future/children side of her apartment. Ch'i entering the room through these windows is met by the ch'i curving around from the hallway. The rug, placed at an angle, guides the energy gently to the bedroom.**

Sitting at her desk, Rosalina looks out onto her living room. The marriage/commitment corner is on the left and the children/creativity wall is straight ahead. The children/creativity wall is also the future wall, and is appropriate for Rosalina's projects, such as the curtains that were designed and made by her especially for these tall windows.

In front of the couch the ch'i from the hallway, now somewhat dispersed, is met by the considerable ch'i from the windows. Generally, more energy is thought to enter a space through the door than the windows, but the power from windows this tall, especially

ABOVE **Future prosperity is symbol-ized on the fame wall by delicate glass flower holders that mimic bamboo.**

RIGHT **The helpful people/travel cor-ner is also known as the father space. The ch'i at this point is moving to the right into the bedroom.**

as light is admitted through the sheer curtains, is enough to balance the ch'i from the hallway and cause it to pause here before gently flowing into the bedroom on the right.

On the fame wall of the living room we placed a very subtle reminder of Rosalina's future aspirations, a delicate flower holder made of individual columns of glass and zinc that resembled bam-boo. Bamboo is thought to be an indication of future prosperity because the new segments between the joints always grow longer than the older ones. Also, we found two Rodin prints dating from 1905. The prints seemed almost a precursor of Rosalina's own style.

On our way to the bedroom we pass the helpful people cor-ner. Here, as in the rest of her apartment, we find fine pieces of highly collectible furniture, such as a chair and ottoman by Hayman Wakefield, a popular furniture manufacturer in the forties and fifties. This is also the father corner where coincidentally Rosalina's boyfriend prefers to sit.

Rosalina's bedroom is the simplest of her rooms. Against the far wall stands Japanese Tansu chests from the early twentieth century, made in Kyoto. The entire area is softened by floor-to-ceiling drapes that cover storage and closet space. This is also the room of an unfortunate accident. On the first day of the Chinese New Year in 1995, Rosalina was preparing food and had opened the metal windows to cool the apartment. Later, when she closed one of the windows, it

Floor-to-ceiling drapes cover the "cutting" edge of the cleaver.

A sharp beam of sunlight is cast by the "cutting" window where Rosalina fractured her fingers. The window is on the cleaver's edge.

slammed down on her fingers. Not only did she mash her fingers, but the window trapped her, and for some time she was unable to raise the window or call for help or even reach a phone. Finally, she wrenched her hand free and went at once to the hospital. The doctor determined that the small bones at the end of two of her fingers were broken. He wanted to put her hand in a cast, but Rosalina would have none of it. She was bandaged and told to be careful.

The story concerned me because of something I had noticed when looking at a floor plan of the apartment: it appeared to be shaped like a cleaver. Apartment shapes such as a cleaver are not necessarily negative. The cleaver is an essential and efficient tool. Still, the entire wall along the living room and bedroom corresponded to the cleaver's edge, and that is where the accident occurred. Floor-to-ceiling curtains like the ones Rosalina had in the bedroom were certainly a step in the right direction. However, the offending window had no cover at all, and so I suggested a drapery that she soon made along with the others in the apartment that covered knife edges and other trouble spots.

Rosalina's kitchen is in the middle of her apartment. According to traditional thinking, the cooking area should be at the edge of the home because of the danger of fire (a fire being more manageable at the edge rather than the center of a house). In fact, an earlier feng shui consultant from Hong Kong, who had made suggestions for Rosalina's apartment from a floor plan, had recommended that she cook as little as possible. It was an unfortunate coincidence that

Rosalina's accident stemmed from cooking. As a result of our consultation she is now more mindful of the fire energy at the center of her home.

Rosalina's apartment has its share of sharp edges, both metaphoric and real. Even in the halls of the building, outside her apartment, the pointed arch is used as a motif. However, with quiet confidence and her own creations she transformed those liabilities into assets. Problems brought about growth, and in growth she positions herself for the next step in a very promising career. Perhaps her next sharp edge will be the leading edge of fashion. ■

The triangular shape of the arch above the counter comes to a point, symbolizing fire, appropriate for the kitchen.

THE MOUNTAIN
AND THE RIVER

Robert Gaul, an interior designer, had recently read about feng shui and applied some of its principles to the renovation of his New York loft. He was particularly interested in comparing his interpretation of his new space with my own. Although I found that he had done an excellent job, the consultation uncovered far more than he had anticipated.

I began with the floor plan, pointing out that the loft was missing a corner. Robert said that it had been cut from the space when the building, located on Printing House Square in lower Manhattan, was divided into co-ops. From a feng shui perspective, missing pieces are not invariably negative (after all, few of us live within perfect squares), but the absence of one or more areas usually has *some* ramifications for the occupants of the space.

I showed Robert how to align the ba-gua by using the entrance to the loft. As a result of this orientation the missing segment turned out to be the knowledge/spirituality corner. (For me, this is a particularly important area in that it brings together both the intellect and the spirit, two concepts often viewed as incompatible.) In this case, the significance of the missing corner was further heightened by the

OPPOSITE The sleeping loft represents the mountain, a metaphor for spirituality, knowledge, and contemplation. The stuffed chicken (it's real) keeps a watchful eye on the entry of the loft.

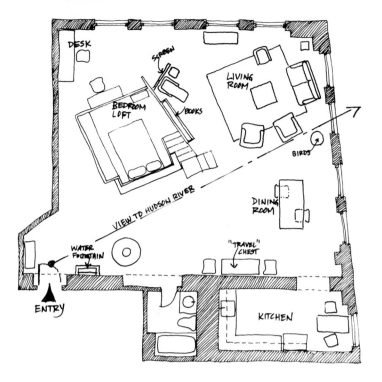

Floor plan illustrating the absence of the knowledge area.

fact that the main entrance to the loft had been located within the cutout area (see the floor plan).

On the ba-gua, the trigram associated with the knowledge/spirituality corner, $\equiv\!\equiv$, is the symbol for "mountain," a place of both meditation and enlightenment. At the time of his renovation Robert, of course, did not realize that it was the knowledge/spirituality area that was missing. Yet strangely, its absence seemed to have guided his hand, for the result was a space of great spirituality. In virtually every nook and cranny I found references to the mountain, and in the middle of the loft . . . there stood a re-creation of the mountain itself.

Like the geomancers who designed the Forbidden City, Robert had built his own mountain where none had existed before, only in this case the mountain was a spacious sleeping loft. Seven feet high, it was easily accommodated by his fourteen-foot ceilings.

The steps leading up the "mountain" were finely crafted drawers inspired by the Japanese Tansu design, just right for his CD collection. The mountain's west side was covered with books and its crest forested by long green leaves of a snake plant. Another side provided access to a storage area (marked by a white curtain) and was presided over by a stuffed chicken that kept an eye on the front door. "Even though the loft platform is inside the larger room," said Robert, "from the top you have a sense of being in a different space with a different perspective. It evokes a separate, calm environment."

From the floor plan you can see that Robert's mountain is not squarely situated in the middle of the loft. If it had been aligned with the walls, it would have blocked light into the entrance foyer. As a result of the loft angle, one can see, immediately on entering the space, light and energy streaming from the tall windows in the southwest corner. Drawn there, one finds a view of the Hudson River. Thus, not only is light conducted into the space more efficiently, but energy is pulled in from the river as well. In fact, the connection is even closer than immediately apparent, as the axis of the bed is parallel to the river itself. Robert's original intention was only to connect his sleeping quarters with some nearby feature of the landscape; he was surprised to note the river was parallel.

Living in balance and harmony with one's surroundings means, at a minimum, that one is aware of those surroundings. Yet most of the residents of Manhattan seem oblivious to the Hudson River, even taken aback when reminded that they live on an island,

Only a sliver of the Hudson River is visible from Robert's loft, and yet the placement of his "mountain," which is aligned with the river, not his building, pulls its energy into his space. River rocks, throughout the apartment, symbolize the river's presence.

OPPOSITE **Light and energy from the window is amplified by the imperial yellow of the walls to enliven the sitting area in the marriage/commitment corner. The rounded, yin features of the French club chairs (ca. 1930) enhance the feeling of comfort and welcome. The hand-tufted rug, "Urban Garden II," was designed by Robert.**

A box below the mirror contains river rocks and a running fountain. Above the frame, gilded rocks symbolize flames. The feather hanging is attached to a Japanese bell that welcomes as well as signals visitors. Stacked boxes on the far wall represent the mountain.

this, despite the river's influence, which is everywhere, dictating the orientation of the major avenues and the island's largest man-made structure, Central Park. Robert sought to connect with these features. About his space he said, "I have created a safe cocoon to live in, and by making focal points of the street, and the river, and even the fountain in the park, I have a connection with the outside and a sense of grounding."

Symbols of the mountain and river appear throughout Robert's apartment. River rocks are the most obvious; stones from the mountain tumbled in streams for millennia until they became the smooth yin shapes familiar to us. In the entrance foyer both mountain and river are graphically reflected in the large mirror/fountain designed by Robert, which he titled "Alchemy." The water, splashing among the stones, greets guests with its welcoming sound and pleasing sight. Along the top of the frame, gilded river stones and sculpted flames add the dimension of fire to the complex work, which rests on a single, large, smooth stone.

In the photograph you see that in the open door a striped feather hangs from a Japanese bell. This is a boundary marker as well as a symbolic warning device. A feather and a bell, of course, do not make an efficient burglar alarm. However, a slight puff of wind on the feather, caused by the opening of the door, will cause the tiny bell to ring. In earlier times, the thoughtful guest touched such a bell to announce his arrival.

Coming into the main area of the loft, we are uplifted by the

The distinctive sculpture provides a welcome focus in the marriage/commitment corner. The red of the love seat produces brilliant contrast to the prevailing yellow. The pattern on the wall is the reflection of sunlight on the tasseled mirror ball.

The birdcage, designed by Robert, is octagonal, symbolizing good luck. Sandblasted glass panels bear the river stone design. Even the color of the finches, Lady Gouldings, echoes the yellow, red, and green color scheme.

vibrant, rich yellow of the walls, which amplifies the light from the tall windows. Sunlight is also reflected off the polished wood floors; in short, energy surges through the space, but it is stilled by the rug, which marks a comfortable sitting area. The palm tree, too, seems to signal this spot as an oasis, a place of rest.

The sitting area shows great care in the selection and placement of objects. The rug, designed by Robert and titled "Urban Garden II," evokes the feel of growing plants and flowers. The sculptured piece in the corner, plaster with glass inlay, provides focus. Primary colors surround it: yellow from the walls, green from the palm, and red from the love seat. So much converges on this spot that the large vintage mirror ball, casually residing on the floor, contributes a welcome dispersal of light and energy.

The octagonal birdcage, again of Robert's design, combines the important motif of river rocks, seen in the glass panels at the base, with natural elements like spiderwebs, and, of course, the birds themselves. Never were little birds—yellow, green, and red—better coordinated with their surroundings. "When I first saw these birds I fell in love with their amazing beauty," Robert explained. "I wanted to create a space equally as beautiful for them. They seem very happy in their home."

Beneath the "mountain" the chaise lounge almost seems nestled in a forest bower. River rocks and spiderwebs on the sand-etched glass of the screen echo the birdcage across the room. Vines and the plant-shaped lamp add even more of nature's forms. According to

In the knowledge corner at the base of the mountain is a chaise lounge. The glass panels of the screen bear the river rock motif and spiderwebs, echoing the birdcage. The cuttings and lamp lend the feeling of a bower.

Robert's desk faces the wall. The cure is three mirrors at eye level that give a view of the entryway. Bubbling water in the round fountain enhances prosperity, and candles pull in positive energy.

We find a Japanese Tansu-style chest designed by Robert at the top of the mountain. An object of beauty at the end of an axis is always good feng shui. The five vases represent the traditional Chinese five elements: earth, fire, metal, wood, and water. The clear squares in the glass provide a frame for the heads of emperor dolls. When the panels are in the open position, as is the one on the left, they frame the round pulls for the drawers, literally placing the "circle in the square" representing heaven and earth.

the ba-gua, we are in the knowledge corner. To the left is Robert's library.

Behind the "mountain," tucked away in the wealth and power corner, we find Robert's office. Above the cabinets, the mountain is re-created in the figures, boxes, and vases. Sand-etched glass panels bear the river rock pattern, and there are also smooth rocks in the fountain, which rests on a work table beneath the window. The water, as ever, enhances prosperity, and the votive candles pull in positive energy. However, note that the desk squarely faces the wall, an improper placement. To compensate, Robert has positioned three different mirrors at eye level to afford multiple views of the entrance to his office. It was also partly because of this placement that the feather and bell were added to the front door. With these alterations the improper placement of the desk is accommodated.

Ascending the stairs to the sleeping platform, we discover at the top a Tansu-style chest constructed of wood, glass, and gold leaf. The revelation of a beautiful object here exemplifies one of the precepts of traditional feng shui landscape design: a garden should not reveal itself all at once. A sense of expectation, even mystery, should be created as to "what's around the next corner." This beautiful piece is also at the end of two axes created by the lines of the top of the planter and the floor, which converge from different directions upon the chest when viewed from the stairs.

Robert designed this chest using the golden mean proportion, also known as the golden section. Thought to have magical properties, this proportion was used in the construction of countless great monuments in the West, such as the Parthenon, and was a favorite design principle of Renaissance architects and painters. The chest was constructed without the use of nails or hardware of any kind. Within the large compartments on either side reside traditional doll effigies of the emperor and his son. When the sliding doors are closed, their heads are framed by the clear squares in the etched glass, or the doors can be moved to the middle to reveal the complete figures.

At last we arrive at the top of the mountain. The proximity of the ceiling, although not oppressive, lends a protective, nurturing feeling to this area. As noted in the photograph, the bed is facing away from both the front door and the ascending platform stairs; this is an improper placement. In this position the bed also faces the large open windows on the south wall, allowing sunlight to affect the rest

The bed in its current position is improperly placed with respect to the stairs that reach the platform on the left. In the past, Robert has turned the bed so that it faces the stairs but found that he rests well in either position. This is because the "mountaintop" has a view of all approaches.

of a late sleeper. In discussions with Robert I learned that he had, in the past, oriented his bed both toward the doors and away from them and seemed comfortable either way. He is an early riser, which means the sunlight is not a problem, and I surmised that the elevation gave him such a strong sense of dominion over his space that specific orientation toward the door was not necessary. "After all," he said, "from the top of the mountain you see all."

Robert's designs are his children, and on the future/children side of the loft we find one of them, a table of deep green granite and steel, which he named the Nassau table after a nearby street. Overhead, a chandelier hangs from a simple covered chain.

On the opposite side of the doorway that leads to the kitchen is the helpful people/travel area, marked by a substantial chest of draw-

OPPOSITE **The dining table, designed by Robert, is made of green marble symbolizing the power of the earth. The chairs display patches of gold leaf for good fortune. A chest of drawers is surrounded by symbols of his travels. The tall candle stand brings positive energy into this area of helpful people and travel.**

The (now) gilded mirror was salvaged from a trash bin. Mirrors are particularly appropriate for the helpful people/travel area, as they open vistas such as the reflected window from across the room.

ers. Displayed on top and on the walls are numerous articles gathered from Robert's travels. The mirror above the chest is garlanded, as is the window in the dining area, creating a visual link between these two focal points.

Coming closer to the helpful people/travel area, we see on top of the chest a multitude of objects presented in a remarkable display of formal clutter. On the wall a symmetrical arrangement of the paintings and prints helps us to both keep track of individual pieces and retain a sense of the overall design. The bilateral symmetry corresponds to the symmetry displayed by our own bodies. In this arrangement the surrounding expanse of brick wall and bare floor also helps to pull together the array, which evokes the fun and enjoyment of travel.

Most people have a collection of objects that evoke memories of beaches, mountains, or distant lands. A grouping of such objects in the travel area acknowledges the importance of these times in our lives and serves to keep alive in us our associations with those places, such as pleasure, relaxation, or simply a sense of the greater world beyond our everyday lives.

The kitchen in this remarkable apartment is small, typically Manhattan; thus, full use is made of the high ceilings with double-decker cabinets and a ladder for access. The sink, unfortunately, is against the far wall and facing away from the entry. Fortunately, glass panels set into the cabinet doors provide a reflective surface almost as effective as mirrors.

The "travel collection" is unified by the round tray on which it rests and the dried bittersweet that forms a protective canopy from above. All the elements are represented. The central statue is a Ming dynasty guardian figure from the Wan-li period.

Although the stove and sink are against the wall, glass panels provide a reflective surface that gives an added sense of security. In traditional feng shui, Robert would be advised to move his knife rack out of the marriage/commitment corner.

At the conclusion of our consultation Robert admitted to having had no central unifying plan with respect to the various references to the mountain and river. At the times when he designed and worked on the loft the spirituality was simply there, he said. "I simply wanted to bring nature and natural forms into my design." It was a desire that he accomplished far more forcefully than he realized. "Now it gives me goose bumps," he said. ∎

8

HOME AND HEARTH

Joanne and Robert Cornog have been renovating their home ever since they were married. Not, however, the *same* home. Every few years they find a new house, settle in, and do what they love best: home renovation. The profit from their passion supplements their income nicely, and for years they have moved smoothly from project to project. But the work on the current object of their attention— a white, two-story cottage on the eastern end of Long Island—never seems to end.

"We can't seem to finish it," Joanne said. "It just goes on and on, and it's draining us financially. At this point we're not sure *what* our plans are anymore."

Joanne is a holistic therapist. Also a dedicated environmentalist, she leads dolphin swims in Florida. Her husband, Robert, is a contractor and designer. His experience and expertise enable them to undertake their extensive renovations at modest cost. This was the first time they had gotten into trouble with one of their projects, and the first time they had sought guidance from feng shui.

Before arriving at any site I usually have an idea of where I want to begin: the client may have mentioned problems relating to a specific area or aspect of the house. But sometimes there are only

OPPOSITE **From his desk in the wealth and power corner Robert oversees the living room, the front door, the stairway to the second floor, and the dining area on the right. Views with wide perspective and depth give a feeling of control and well-being.**

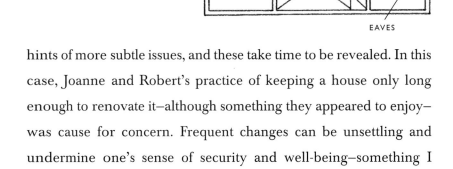

ROBERT'S DESK

LOVESEAT

The first floor. The new position of Robert's desk gives maximum perspective of major features of the interior of the house, good strategy given the Cornogs' objectives.

FORMER GARAGE

FORMER LOCATION OF ROBERT'S DESK

ENTRANCE

EAVES

The second floor. Moving the master bed farther out from beneath the eaves was crucial in changing the Cornogs' feelings about the bedroom.

EAVES

hints of more subtle issues, and these take time to be revealed. In this case, Joanne and Robert's practice of keeping a house only long enough to renovate it—although something they appeared to enjoy—was cause for concern. Frequent changes can be unsettling and undermine one's sense of security and well-being—something I would watch for in the coming consultation.

Since money was an immediate problem, I began by checking the position of Robert's desk, which he had located in the knowledge corner of the living room. It did not matter that the desk was largely symbolic (Robert manages his design company from an office); its placement in his home reflected a personal perspective on his work. It also offered an appealing view of the front garden and driveway.

The knowledge corner is a suitable location for a desk. And a good view is ordinarily an asset, too, but in this case Robert may have spent too much time looking off into the distance—perhaps to his next project—instead of concentrating on the work at hand. The absolutely best position for a desk is the wealth and power corner. My recommendation was that Robert relocate his desk to that position and turn it so that he would have a complete view of the living room. Other major areas of the apartment that would also be in his direct line of sight were the front door, the stairway to the loft, the dining area, and the hearth. With this change Robert's visual domain expanded to include critical areas of the home and thus enhanced his feeling of mastery of his environment. Perhaps it would also serve as a reminder to finish the job at hand.

A major element of the Cornogs' renovation (and one that had not yet been undertaken) was the relocation of the master bedroom from the second floor to the former garage on the west side of the house. I counseled strongly against this move. Their existing bedroom was on the marriage/relationship side of the house, a strong position from a feng shui point of view. Moreover, their plans downstairs included a kitchen next to the breezeway adjacent to the garage. I pointed out that kitchens, by their very nature, are dynamic. People congregate there. Conversation and the bustle of preparing meals can make them noisy at any hour. The active, yang energy of such a room could be disruptive to anyone trying to rest in the adjacent bedroom. Also, the kitchen would completely divide

In the entryway an antiqued mirror provides an element of security. On the future side of the foyer, the mirror also welcomes guests, as does the potpourri in the porcelain bowl.

The new office, converted from a garage, makes use of a fence to deflect the negative energy of automobiles from the driveway. A gravel walk leads the visitor to the front door.

OPPOSITE A love seat appears to extend the downstairs bedroom (on the right) into the end of a sun-dappled loggia. The quarry-tile floor and ficus trees lend an outdoor feeling, while the sculptured dolphins symbolize Joanne's commitment to ecology.

the master bedroom, and thus the couple, from the rest of the home. I felt this could cause problems for their family; for instance, their children might feel the separation from their parents.

Another problem with moving the master bedroom into the garage was created by the long, curved driveway. Although it now stopped short of the house, it nevertheless seemed to convey the energy from approaching automobiles directly into the soon-to-be bedroom. This would scarcely be conducive to sleep. Robert had sensed this problem several weeks before our consultation and installed a fence directly in front of the garage to shield it from the headlights and noise of oncoming cars, but it was not enough.

I asked if perhaps the small downstairs bedroom would be big enough for the two of them. "Relative to the ba-gua, this is your marriage corner," I explained, "and the bedroom could be extended into this end of the loggia by a love seat, or other pieces that symbolize a couple."

The Cornogs decided that the downstairs bedroom was too small for the two of them. They did, however, act upon my recommendation, in part, by furnishing the loggia with a comfortable love seat and two large ficus trees. This arrangement created an oasis, a place of rest from the constant construction taking place in their home. (At the time, the garage renovation and part of the loggia were yet to be finished.)

What to do with the garage? Once incorporated into the living space, it would constitute the entire west end of the house, and thus

encompass three major areas as represented on the ba-gua: wealth and power, family, and knowledge. My first suggestion was to convert the room into an office, an appropriate use of the knowledge and wealth and power areas. Clients could then enter Robert's place of business without going through the living quarters. Alternatively, I suggested a family room, doubly appropriate since wealth and power could be reinterpreted as the wealth of the family.

The Cornogs decided to turn the garage into an office. The energy from the driveway, they reasoned, would be more easily subsumed in daytime office activity. Once made, that decision meant that the master bedroom would have to remain where it was. Now we needed to address the conditions that were making that room uncomfortable, namely, the slanted eaves. "It feels like the room is coming down on us," Joanne said when we returned to the second floor. "We're getting all this pressure."

Slanted overhangs can impose a feeling of pressure and intrusion. The bed was angled from the corner in order to create space on both sides. A console table placed at its head holds two lamps, a symbol of relationship.

I proposed two solutions. First, the bed was repositioned as shown in the photograph, so that there was space on either side. Having no space on one side of a bed symbolizes a one-sided relationship and can create resentment or add to any tensions that already exist. Also, with the bed extended farther out into the room, it did not seem to be so oppressed by the eaves. Next, we installed a table behind the bed: its twin lamps served as a cure. The photographs in pairs mounted between the windows symbolized the couple's marriage commitment.

Moving the bed to this new position meant, however, that an overhead beam now hung above one of the sleepers. In traditional feng shui, such a configuration is thought to cause problems with the part of the body over which the beam passes. Should they begin to feel any discomfort in the newly positioned bed, I counseled, they should hang a round, faceted crystal on nine inches of red silk from

On the second floor, as on the first, consistent placement of the desk in the wealth and power corner reinforces the couple's financial priorities. Here, too, the guest bed is angled from the wall to create space on both sides.

The treelike branching of beams gives the dining area the feeling of a sheltered bower. An angel warming his feet on the mantel is an icon of protection. The symbols on the porcelain urns read "double happiness."

the offending beam. In traditional thinking, a crystal transforms negative energy into a healing rainbow of colors. Another remedy would be to hang two bamboo flutes—one at either end—from the overhead beam. I also suggested that painting the beams white to match the ceiling would lessen their oppressive ch'i.

The room at the other end of the loft area was Joanne's study, which also served as a guest room. Her desk was in the marriage corner—a practical location, symbolizing Joanne's commitment to her work. However, I suggested she move it to the wealth and power corner. That would mirror her husband's desk placement downstairs and thus doubly reinforce the couple's first goal of overcoming their financial problems. Meanwhile, the far right corner of the room, the marriage and commitment corner, was a good place for a bed—even a guest bed.

Overhead beams were also a feature of this room, and one crossed the guest bed in its new location. The remedies I suggested earlier for their master bedroom would work equally well here, but instead of a crystal or bamboo flutes, Joanne mounted two small angels on the beam above the bed. This was an excellent solution since in the West angels are traditional icons of protection.

In my discussions with the Cornogs it became clear that they had not neglected their personal relationship in the face of the continual renovations. Their extensive use of candlelight was perhaps the most tangible evidence of this. They had collected many different types of candelabra, votives, and candlesticks. Even in the foyer a wrought-iron candle chandelier had been installed. Candlelight always promotes positive energy and is a universal symbol of romance and intimacy.

Today, the use of candles is always noted and perceived as purposeful because they require so much more effort and attention than electric lights. Equally important is the fireplace, which the Cornogs always lit, even in the spring and the fall. Long a symbol of nurturing, the hearth serves also as a symbol of the safety of home. Perhaps this dates to distant times when fire kept more than just the cold away and was, in itself, a form of security.

The warmth of candlelight and wood creates an intimate yin space beneath the loft overhang. Plants soften the edges of beams, and the absence of artificial light in the double-height space helps to preserve the atmosphere.

The couple marks the changing seasons by shifting the living and dining room furniture. In summer, when their home was photographed, the couches are always placed in the sunlit loggia adjacent to the kitchen, and the fireplace enhances the intimate dining area. During the winter the couches are returned to the living room, cozy with the glowing fireplace, while the dining area in the loggia takes advantage, during the day, of the winter sun.

Toward the end of the consultation I sensed that Robert and Joanne still felt that something about their space remained unresolved. I asked about the history of the house. Who were the former owners? What happened to them? Their reaction made it clear that I had touched upon a troubling aspect of the property.

They had purchased the house from a developer who was in financial difficulty. According to feng shui, property acquired under adverse circumstances brings those problems along with it. In this case the developer was still financially involved with the renovations, and he frequently appeared at the house to inspect the work. Because of his continuing association, the man felt free to examine the property at any time, and Joanne never knew when she would find him there.

Joanne felt helpless during these unannounced visits, almost violated—as if she and Robert didn't really have control of their own home. I suggested having a blessing ceremony. The troubles of the couple were not so much with the physical space in which they lived—it was, after all, a beautiful house—but their *feeling* about that

The red envelopes contain the Cornogs' wishes as expressed in the blessing ceremony. Now placed in a bowl, they guard a trapdoor in the kitchen's wealth and power corner.

space. The changes I had proposed served as markers of their intentions, but the ceremony would also require them to articulate those intentions, expressing them concretely both to me and to one another. This extra attention, which they felt they needed, acknowledged and reinforced their resolve, and brought all their aspirations into focus with a single act.

A few weeks later we performed a feng shui blessing ceremony to release the home from negative influences of the past, and to acknowledge the couple's intentions as represented by the changes they were making. During the ceremony, deep feelings were touched. There were even tears.

Two weeks later I received a call from Joanne, who told me about a curious incident. In the interval since the blessing ceremony, the developer had come again to the house—unannounced, as usual. This particular time she saw him from the window, walking to the front door—where suddenly he paused. Then he knocked at the front door, which he had never done before. He had an odd, almost uncomfortable expression on his face when Joanne answered. And, instead of prying to the point of intrusion, he cursorily examined the premises, expressed his approval, and left.

Joanne was triumphant. Although he had not said a word, the man had tacitly acknowledged their ownership of the space. Perhaps he had sensed something different, another presence, or perhaps it was just the accumulated changes. Whatever it was, Joanne knew, at last, that the house was theirs. ∎

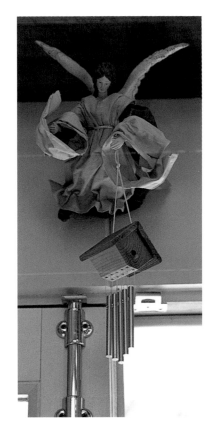

Wind chimes at entry points enhance security, since the breeze from an opened door can signal arrivals. They also welcome friends who enter the space. Here an angel guards the door.

9

AN AMERICAN
GEOMANCER

When Anton began searching for a house, he knew nothing of feng shui, only that he wanted a very particular view of the Hudson River. "I wanted a home that reflected the feeling of the valley I grew up in," he said, "so that meant a view of the river, but also I wanted the kind of view you would get from a boat: I wanted to look *down* the river, not across it." Starting out with geodetic survey maps, Anton worked his way up the Hudson. At Croton, where the river makes a sharp turn to the west, he knew he could find the view he wanted.

In the beginning Anton worked with topological maps, which show precise features of the land. This was important because elevation wasn't the only consideration; the site had to slope steeply enough so that trees did not obscure the view. After pinpointing several places that might have all the desired characteristics, he studied a county road map and began looking for access into these areas.

The most beneficial river site, in feng shui terms, is on either side, preferably on the inside of an arc or curve, a position known as the "belly of the dragon." A river flowing away from a house, a site such as Anton sought, is a classic example of bad feng shui. Such a river is thought to drain the site too quickly of its beneficial ch'i.

Windows in the living room look out onto an ideal southern view that includes the low-lying Hudson River Valley and, of course, the river itself in the distance. Such a view is known as the red phoenix.

OPPOSITE The calm boat basin collects ch'i and serves as a buffer between the house and the Hudson. Since the river is tidal, it can carry ch'i in either direction.

Seeking a downriver view, the owner discovered the site with the aid of geodetic survey maps.

Anton's site, however, not only possessed the view he required but was positioned so that a remarkable confluence of the topography corrected its negative aspects. First, the Hudson at Croton widens dramatically and becomes quite shallow, with an average depth of only seventeen feet. This means the flow of energy away from the house is considerably slowed. Places where ch'i is slowed (but not stopped) are very beneficial. Second, there is a small bay at the bend in the river, where the water is noticeably calmer. Inlets and bays often form small pockets, draining off and calming ch'i from the main flow. In this case even the boaters on the river seemed drawn to such a beneficial concentration of ch'i. Frequently, Anton said, he looked down from his house to see boats gathered in the bay.

The third remarkable aspect of the site is that the Hudson is tidal, meaning that the river, near the ocean, responds to the ocean's rise and fall. (The Indian name for the Hudson, Muhheakunnuk, means the river that flows both ways.) Thus, sometimes the river flows away from the house, sometimes toward it, and sometimes, while changing direction, it is relatively still. To have a river flowing straight *toward* a house is problematic because it delivers the ch'i too quickly, changing its benevolence into poison arrows. But here the boat basin protects Anton's site, buffering it from the excess of energy flowing, in this case, upstream.

Anton's site is no less remarkable than the river: the house has a hill to its back, smaller hills on either side, and a view of lower-lying valley to the south. In feng shui terms such a configuration is perfect.

The mountain in back of the house is known as the black tortoise; the hills are the white tiger to the west and the green dragon to the east, and the view to the south is the red phoenix. Even from a contemporary ecological standpoint it is a very strong site. The house is well protected from blizzards from the north, and its elevation means that there is no danger of flooding. The mountain in back (actually a hill) is gentle and sloping, so there is little danger of landslide or erosion. And finally, the configuration is open to the beneficial ch'i from the south, which includes the warmer southern breezes, and sunshine, even in winter.

In approaching the house, I noted that the front door is on the north side, meaning the entrance occurs on what should be the owner's protected side. Ideally, the entrance should have been on the south, with the road coming from below. (Such an approach would have been logical in premechanical times when animal-powered wagons would be strained by an incline.) The access road to Anton's site was, however, from the crest of the hill, but it did not approach the house directly. Instead, it wound its way through a wooded area to the west, by a pond, and partway down the hill before turning back up to Anton's house. It was almost as if someone had consciously wanted to satisfy the feng shui prescription and taken the road back down the hill so as to approach the house from the south. Even its curves were good feng shui. (There is a saying in China that only armies and bandits move in straight lines.) Eventually, Anton's drive went around the house and into a garage

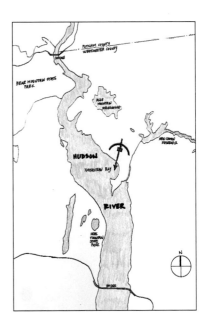

Map showing the excellent feng shui siting of this house with its armchair configuration and southern exposure.

Like guardians, two trees stand at the entrance to the house.

that was separate from the main structure. The garage, too, faced south, a correct entry.

I asked Anton how he felt about the house in terms of security. He said that his land was buffered by the properties of his neighbors with whom he had excellent relations. Also, the dirt access road was unmarked, giving him little traffic, but when anyone did approach, he always heard them because of the roundabout route. He then pointed out two trees, one on either side of the walkway to the house proper. He had always regarded these trees as sentinels, symbolically guarding the entry.

All the features Anton pointed out were relevant in feng shui terms. Added to the guardian trees (particularly important) was the circuitous path of the drive and the fact that cars entered the garage from the south. Combined, these features constituted what I felt was the minimal correction necessary for the northern entry into the house. However, as I was soon to discover, the problem of an incorrect entryway was to arise again in another guise.

Anton's bedroom, on the second floor, is open to the magnificent view to the south. The low platform bed is positioned in the middle of the room, away from the wall, and the built-in lighting around the bed is symmetrical. This arrangement re-creates, in miniature, both the virtues and the problems of the overall site. The bed has no headboard, so the sleeper is completely unprotected. Usually the head of the bed would be against a wall, *particularly* if it had no headboard, and ideally it would be a protected wall. His vulnerability is

compounded by the fact that the door enters into the room from behind the bed, the worst possible position. The sleeper is subject to unexpected events. But again, Anton was adamant about his feeling for the space. "Having something behind you and feeling that you are protected is all relative to what you have in front," he said. "This house has so much energy coming toward it . . . at night I can see the Empire State Building, the Chrysler Building, and the expanse of the Tappan Zee Bridge like a queen's necklace, across the night river. There's so much energy out there that one gets the sense that the

Even from the foyer one can look through to the fame wall and the spectacular view of the Hudson River Valley. One feels the closeness of the house (yin) contrasting with the expansiveness of the outdoors (yang).

The "armchair" formation of the overall site (the bed represents the house) is reflected in the master bedroom. But the entry, from where the photograph is taken, is from the back, as is the exterior approach to the house, presenting problems.

entire world is before you and nothing at all behind you. In fact, there's another row of bedrooms back there, across the hall, that buffer me. And besides, my bed has enough of a back and sides that I have a sense of being nestled when I go to sleep."

It was an interesting problem, and one that I had seen before. The room was oriented toward an impressive view, and its entrance was from behind. It was the same for the house. The view was to the south, the front door on the north. Anton's feelings were strong on the subject, and he did have some reasonable feng shui perspectives with which to back his views. And why not? He had prospered in his space. His own ch'i was sufficient to withstand levels of energy that would have overcome many people. Yet unexpected events, even tragedy, had also found him out. Five years after buying this house his wife was killed in an automobile accident. Her loss was a terrible blow to him; he spoke of her repeatedly and fondly. Eventually, he regained his equilibrium. Life went on. In the bedroom one could see evidence of that balance, even with the improper entrance. The bed was exactly in the center of the room; the two matching light fixtures, left and right, were symmetrically arranged, as were the windows.

There was also evidence of tentative new beginnings in the bedroom. On the future side, on top of a beautiful built-in cabinet, rested a superb sound system, a gift from the new woman in his life. Above the CD player a round mirror connoted wholeness and compassion. A tiny gold picture frame sat on the cabinet surface.

Stepping into the master bath, we saw again the beautiful view to the south. Double sinks, on either side of a window, faced the same direction. Above the sinks, the mirrors were positioned so that they brought all the energy of the red phoenix, reflecting off a mirror on the back wall and out the window, to the occupants even as they brushed their teeth.

The library on the second floor is in the marriage/relationship corner. The most yin of all the rooms, it is one of the few inward-looking spaces in the house. A manteled fireplace on the west wall dominates the room, further emphasizing warmth. A striking art photograph of two figures selected by Anton's wife hangs over the fireplace. Lighting from both above and below gives it an ethereal appearance. "At the end of the day we often ended up in this room," he says, glancing at the two chairs before the fireplace. Her ashes rest nearby in a beautiful urn.

On the future side, a large round mirror connotes love and compassion. The sound system was a gift, the result of a new relationship, but a little gold frame near the window remains empty.

A window can provide a beautiful view, but it does not necessarily relieve the cramped feeling of a small space. Strategically placed mirrors not only make the room seem larger, but pull beneficial ch'i from the outdoors.

OPPOSITE The library, which is used in the evening, is the only room on the south side of the house that does not emphasize the river view. Its fireplace creates a warm yin space, contrasting with the yang or outward focus of the other rooms.

An opening in a hedge (known as the "mouse hole") creates a sense of curiosity and expectation.

Outside, at the point where the flagstone walkway curved into the house, we found an intriguing opening in the hedge (Anton called it a "mouse hole") that formed a quiet, yin entrance to a stone pathway. We were in the knowledge and spirituality area of the property, and the meadow to which this little path led was one of the most secluded places on the site.

Continuing around the edge of the house, we came to a striking view that reflected the balance in Anton's life as much as any room or furniture arrangement: it was an exterior view of all three floors of the house's wealth and power corner. Anton has had con-

siderable success as an engineer, designer, and inventor. His company presently manufactures vital components for film and video. The top floor, with its expansive windows, is an extension off the master bedroom. It is where Anton keeps some of his collection of toy locomotives. For Anton, the locomotive is tied inextricably to the spirit of the Hudson Valley. The railroad brought industry; it created convenient access from New York City and turned country hills into retreats for the privileged class. Bringing commerce and prestige, the railroad was the energizer of the valley, an active, yang enterprise.

Contour map showing classical feng shui elements in armchair configuration.

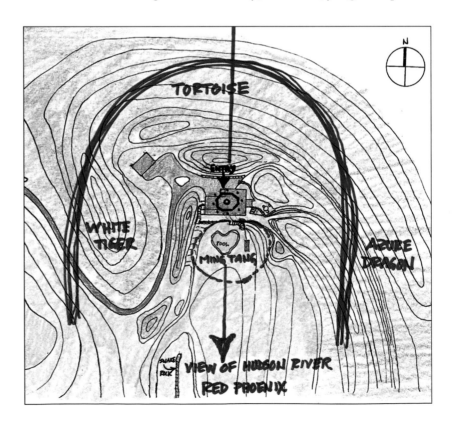

When he is at home, Anton does most of his work on the second floor in the wealth and power corner. No high-powered office, this corner is actually an extension of his kitchen. Here he can deal with the many and complex issues that comprise his life in a homey, down-to-earth atmosphere.

The ground floor is a much more yin space than the other two floors. Containing only one window on the east side, it is clearly not outward-looking. Designed especially for listening to music, it is primarily a place of contemplation and comfort, though it is also wired as a disco. Despite the special lighting effects, symbolically the black walls are turned inward. (Black is the ultimate yin color.) One has the feeling of another dimension created for music and movement, but it is a dimension circumscribed by the walls of the room.

Balance is the key to managing a site of great energy. For their office, most people would have taken the top floor, with the best perspective and magnificent view. The intensely private might have squirreled away their workroom on the ground floor like a nest. But this man of symmetry chose the middle, between these two extremes. From a position of stability, between the yang of the top floor and the yin of the bottom floor, Anton reaches out as a businessman, an inventor, an engineer.

Anton's swimming pool is located at the bottom of his site in the central position, or Ming Tang, between the protective arms of the white tiger and the green dragon. Stone stairs wind down to the pool, emphasizing the protective, nurturing aspect of the location

The office is on the middle floor, neither the most expansive yang position (the top floor) nor the most enclosed yin position (the bottom floor).

Traditional elements can be used to create balance and harmony. In the living room, a group of metals on a low table provide relief from the wood that dominates the room.

and channeling the ch'i from the hilltop gently to the Ming Tang below. At first glance, the pool seems free-form, but in fact the shape is a replica of the Hudson just below his property; thus, symbolically, the energy of the river is brought up into this protected grove.

The Ming Tang, the center position of the ba-gua, represents the self. It is also the position for health. Anton heats the pool, and so is able to use it late into the fall and early in the spring as a place of therapy as well as enjoyment. On this October day steam rose from the still surface—it seemed an enchanted place, a magic pool within a sacred grove. At night he can watch the stars while relaxing in the warm water. Anton uses no lights at night; indeed, he has painted the pool black so that at night the focus of the swimmer is outward toward the stars or to the distant glow of New York City. The trees on either side lift their branches as if to shelter all within this space.

The pool broadly reproduces the form that the Hudson takes just below this site.

On the white tiger side of the site (the east side), there is yet another pool some distance away, this one a quiet forest pond. A meditative place, it is a favorite of Anton's and a focus for local wildlife, including deer (which he knows individually), raccoons, birds, and a resident groundhog.

The grounds had been his wife's domain; gardening her passion. After her death Anton began a systematic exploration of the land, giving himself hands-on tasks to fill his time. He discovered that he enjoyed the labor, uncovering vestiges of work that had been done previously on the site. One of his most propitious finds was a wall/rock formation that he dubbed "snake rock." It was part of an early stone wall, probably nineteenth-century. Removing the thick underbrush and small trees, he carefully restored it. Some fifty or sixty feet

long, its shape suggesting a snake, a large rock marking the head. It was an appropriate find. In feng shui the snake is a metaphor for transition. Anton can see it when he looks out from the windows of his house. For him, transition is not the only answer, but it is the best one.

When I returned for a second visit, I reviewed again the questions I had about this remarkable site. Would Anton's willpower and positive view continue to sustain him in a place of such high energy? Were his own feng shui analyses sufficient to retain the balance that he so obviously desired? Seldom had I seen a site with such spectacular strengths and potentially dangerous weaknesses; Anton with his force of character was the man to manage them. ■

10

D U N E   C A S T L E

The owners of this luxurious waterfront site were first introduced to feng shui by the interior designer Eugenia Au Kim, who had already redesigned a large portion of the house. Privacy, Eugenia explained, was a major concern of the owners, but they were, however, happy to offer a view of the renovations to date, all of which they felt sustained the harmony and peace of the site as it evolved.

I was asked to do a feng shui consultation in order to provide an in-depth perspective and to contribute to what the owners hoped would be a master plan for future architectural and interior changes. The home was not originally built with feng shui principles in mind; therefore, the photographs show places yet to be corrected, as well as feng shui innovations designed by Eugenia, already in place.

From the road you can see little of this remote and comfortable hideaway, only a bit of the second story and a yellow chimney by which the house is known, since it has no street address. Not until you come to a stop in the driveway do you discover an unassuming stairway of bleached timbers. Climbing past potted geraniums and petunias, one arrives at a comfortable porch and the somewhat more formidable white walls of the house. The solid planting of evergreens that envelopes this part of the site provides the classic feng shui

Weathered stairs lead to an outdoor sitting area and porch. The surrounding evergreens create a traditional feng shui barrier against negative ch'i and screen out noise from the road.

OPPOSITE **An overhead extension from the master bedroom provides direct access to the beach and the other side of the pool. Viewed from the metaphor of the "castle," it is the drawbridge.**

The old-fashioned porch that greets us at the top of the stairs serves as a halfway station between the contemporary interior we are about to enter and the natural feeling of the evergreens beyond. The owners watch birds from this vantage point.

My working sketch showing the bagua areas.

shield from negative ch'i, which, in this case, includes noise from the nearby road. It also screens the house from the eyes of the curious.

It was in this quiet, outdoor sitting area, with its natural wood deck and unpainted furniture, that the owner was waiting for me. He loved to sit here, he said, and watch the birds and other wildlife attracted by the shelter of the trees, the birdhouses, and the feeder. Abundant wildlife, I told him, is always a sign of good ch'i.

Entering the house proper, I found myself facing a wall not more than three feet in front of the door. Such an obvious obstacle this close to an entrance implies barriers or obstructions in one's life. When I mentioned this to the owner, he admitted to never being happy with this configuration himself, and we began discussing design solutions that would create an open, welcome feeling.

Another problem resulting from the wall was a phenomenon

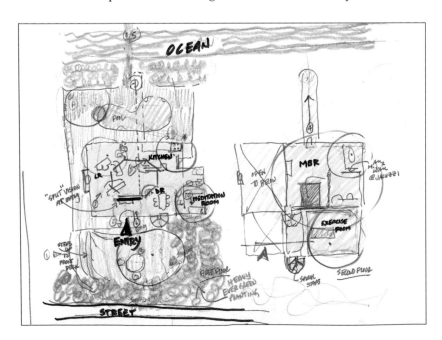

An example of split vision, the front door enters directly onto the close wall on the right. The narrow table and plant soften the effect and provide near-at-hand focus as one moves through the narrow space.

known as split vision, created when a nearby wall only *partially* obstructs the view. If the distant focus is interesting and the near wall dull, the eye hesitates a moment, preferring the distant perspective, yet the near wall must be taken in as well (at the very least so as to be avoided). The cure? Give the eye a nearby reference point. In the present case a table had been placed in front of the offending wall, with a ceramic bird and a period water jug on top. I suggested adding something at eye level like a painting or a photograph until the wall was removed. I also recommended a plant at the edge of the wall to soften the knife edge one passed when entering the living room.

The living room is in the wealth and power corner of the house, which, in feng shui terms, is an indication that friends and family are held in high esteem. Overall, I found the space had an expansive, yang feeling, with its high white walls, big windows, and light gray floor. On the other hand, the clustering of the furniture around the

OPPOSITE **The eight-sided ba-gua is re-created in this arrangement. The position of the chairs and couches form the "corners," while the walls of the room represent its cardinal sides. The ba-gua shape itself is seen in the black medallion on the rug. The round table forms the yin-yang balance of the center.**

The kitchen, in the marriage/relationship corner, nestles behind a curved, yin counter. The round mirror mounted on a copper square base acknowledges an incorrect placement of the stove.

fireplace created a comfortable, yin enclosure within the larger space, in part because the couches and chairs were arranged so that they mimicked the ba-gua—a particularly auspicious shape. The eight-sided figure was also reflected in the pattern of the contemporary Oriental rug.

The kitchen is in the marriage/relationship corner behind a curved white tile counter. A door in the corner leading to the pantry was painted yellow, providing a clever focus for the eye. Unfortunately, the stove had been placed next to the yellow door (against the outer wall), so when the oven door was open, passage was completely blocked. Neither entryways nor stoves should be cramped, and traditional wisdom attributes all kinds of malady to restrictions around the stove. Even the family's health can be at risk since the cook will be inconvenienced. The owners could not move the stove immediately, and so a mirror was placed on the adjacent wall as a temporary acknowledgment of the problem. "Acknowledging" a problem with a cure is a relatively weak way of addressing it. In this case the mirror was too high to give a feeling of increased space around the stove. The main value of such a cure is in the awareness that it creates by marking or reminding one of the problem. For a future renovation, the owners discussed the possibility of relocating the stove to the end of the opposite counter so that the door opens into the kitchen and the person cooking faces the dining room.

The curved kitchen counter was mirrored above by a curved overhead beam that emphasized the yin nature of the enclosure. The

The walkway from the beach is slightly offset from the overhead extension across the pool, thus slowing the approach of energy from the ocean. A curved walkway would have been even better.

beam was not problematic because it was not directly above the occupants when they were seated at the counter. A beautiful bonsai tree, the traditional symbol of longevity, rested on the countertop. Beneath the windows was a red lamp providing task-specific lighting.

In back of the house was the pool with its soft, curved contours. In the nearby wealth and power corner a round Jacuzzi bubbled merrily. Moving water connotes prosperity (although care must be taken with any water appliance, because problems such as leaking pipes are thought to affect one's finances). The most impressive feature, however, was an imposing overhead walkway that extended from the fame side of the house over the pool, providing direct access to the beach walk from the upstairs master bedroom. This extension, if it had been narrower, could have had the negative energy of an overhead beam. However, it was actually wide enough to serve as a porch or balcony, and the spiral staircase at its end energized the far side of the pool. For a while I was puzzled as to why this striking overhead appendage should be so satisfying. After all, a stairway from the second-floor bedroom could have descended directly to the deck without first crossing the swimming pool. Of course, access to the water is vitally important in a beach house, but it would not have been so terrible to walk around the pool on the way to the beach. Not until later, when thinking about the privacy and protection aspect of the house, did I realize another psychological aspect to the overhead walkway. The long and narrow appendage spanning the water had the feel of a drawbridge extending out over the moat

The warmth of the beige walls, the softness of the pillows and thick carpet, and an excellent sound system cushion the senses in the meditation room. High windows admit light but prevent visual distraction, encouraging contemplation in this simple yin space

of a medieval castle. The image was consistent with other protective features of the house, including the heavy planting of trees, the formidable front walls of the house, the "walls" created by the dunes, and, of course, the symbolic moat of the swimming pool.

Beyond the pool a wooden walkway gave access to the beach across the overgrown swale. It was not in line with the overhead walkway that traversed the pool, so the energy either way from the beach or the house was slowed. This was important. Movement of ch'i from a house too quickly could drain it of luck and good fortune. Conversely, movement of the ocean's ch'i too quickly toward the house could increase its vulnerability to the sea's destructive force. Abundant vegetation also provided some general cover from the energy of the sea.

The ocean and the pool were not the only dominant features of the house. A meditation room was located in a front corner of the ground floor. High windows gave a sense of privacy. Heavy carpet and an excellent sound system cushioned any but the loudest intru-

Bright colors direct the ch'i along the spiral staircase as one ascends to the second floor.

The center of the house, the position of self and health, is energized by two domed skylights. Seven-foot giraffes preside over the gallery above the living room.

sions from the outside. This was a favorite space of the owners, where even the energy of the ocean seemed remote. A single potted orchid and a photograph of a Buddhist monk created a thoughtful and meditative atmosphere. This room, in the helpful people corner, was where his mother stayed on her frequent visits.

I observed that small windows were characteristic of all the rooms on the front side of the house, which is typical of most modern beach houses that open themselves with huge picture windows and glass doors to the prevailing ch'i of the ocean while at the same time presenting a blank front to passersby behind them. A feng shui analysis of such houses can be complex, as more energy tends to enter these houses from the ocean side than from the front door.

Wide, spiral stairs painted in bright colors led to the second floor. Big and round, they gave one the feeling of climbing a castle turret. When I inquired about the unusual color scheme, the owner said that when going up and down stairs, he believed one's focus should be solely on the stairs. For that reason he placed nothing on the surrounding walls to distract, leaving only the steps as the focal point. In feng shui, open spiral stairs are thought to affect one's health negatively, but I felt that here the stairs, with their closed risers and no distractions for the eye, managed the ch'i both comfortably and carefully. Of course, bright colors have connotations, such as playfulness, and that added to the energy of the second floor.

In the gallery, overlooking the living room, the menagerie idea from downstairs continued in the two very striking wooden giraffes from Zimbabwe. More than seven feet tall, these arresting figures gave an air of fantasy to the house. Above them, one of two domed skylights brought natural light onto these airy creatures and into the heart of the home. The skylights were circular, appropriate for the center of the house, and they were properly placed, that is, not over a major piece of furniture or a bed. For most people, skylights allow too much energy to be concentrated above a sleeping area or some other place where they would spend a major amount of time.

One of the most unusual spots in this remarkable house was the exercise room, which balanced extreme expressions of yin and yang. The owners were shocked when Eugenia suggested they paint the room black. Black is the ultimate yin color. Black is also the color associated with career, and this room, appropriately, is on the career side of the house. Large windows looking onto the dunes and the beach provide relief from the closed-in yin feeling of the black, but Eugenia also added floor-to-ceiling mirrors on one wall. Mirrors reduce stress by providing more distant focal points, and in this case they also opened the room even more to the outside view from the windows. Thus the room balanced the yin feeling of the black walls with the open, expansive, and yang feeling of the large mirrors and windows. The engaging focus on nature also made the room very satisfying to use because the mind could be occupied while the body was being exercised.

Entering the master bedroom, I was struck again with the animal motif. Two monkeys formed the arms and back of a graceful

The exercise room balances the black of the walls and floor (yin) with the light and the view from the windows (yang). Both are given depth by their reflection in the floor-to-ceiling mirrors.

As is the case with many beach houses, the primary source of ch'i is from the ocean rather than through the doorway in which we are standing. The weight of the two chests anchors the otherwise yang expanse of the room.

wrought-iron chair. In this household, I was assured, wildlife was more than a decoration. The owners were dedicated to the preservation of ecological habitats and took great delight in playful references to wild places.

From the door of the bedroom one looked past the monkey chair to the balcony that extended over the swimming pool. This vantage point gave me a sense of being directly attached to the ocean, an umbilical cord to the source of incredible natural strength and power. From a feng shui point of view, the extension was on the fame side, connoting perhaps the single most desirable attribute of any house in this exclusive area: direct access to the beach.

Bedrooms are, of course, usually yin places, enclosed and protected. This bedroom was an exception, opening itself to the splendors of its location. This is because it is a beach house, of course, but still *some* yin grounding was necessary. Two solid pieces of furniture provided that grounding. One was a tall chest of drawers and the other was a storage chest with brass fixtures. Both were of dark wood and gave the impression of being quite heavy. Their weight and stability provided a welcome contrast to the otherwise consistent expansiveness of the room.

On the other side of the bedroom was another Jacuzzi, this one in the marriage/relationship corner. It had a spectacular view of the ocean, complete with windows, mirrors, and a glass wall. Beautiful vistas are always calming to the spirit.

I saved consideration of the bed for last. It was on the right, as you enter the room, its head against the same wall as the door, which is *very* incorrect feng shui. Yet the circumstances of this house were so unique that further analysis was necessary.

To create a place that is maximally conducive to rest, a bedroom should be treated as if it were a small-scale reproduction of the classical ideal feng shui home site. In that formation a house is situated on the south side of a mountain and should also face south, providing the greatest protection from the north wind; smaller hills should extend from either side of the mountain to provide protective arms. The imagery for this configuration is the black turtle (the mountain to the north), the azure dragon (the hills to the east), and the white tiger (the hills to the west). The only easy avenue for ch'i to approach is from the south, which means only the most beneficial weather, prevailing winds, sunlight, and so forth.

In the bedroom, by analogy, the head of the bed should be

A Jacuzzi off the master bedroom (and in the marriage/relationship corner) is enhanced by a mirror wall that doubles the view.

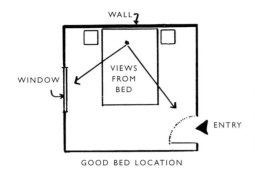

WALL

WINDOW

VIEWS FROM BED

ENTRY

GOOD BED LOCATION

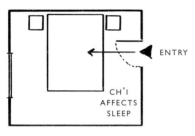

ENTRY

CH'I AFFECTS SLEEP

POOR BED LOCATION

TOP **The head of the bed should be against the most protected wall (the mountain), and doors should be from the symbolic south, either on the opposite wall or on the side walls close to the far corners.**

ABOVE **A door alongside the bed has the potential of broadsiding the sleeper with energy that could disturb sleep.**

The large painting above the bed connotes a mystic circle of welcoming figures of which the viewer seems to be a part. The photographs of the chimpanzees and people represent the owners' belief that all creatures share equally in the circle of life.

against the most protected wall (the black turtle). The walls on either side should provide subordinate protection, and the only entrance for ch'i should be from the opposite end of the room. Thus doors (which, in a room, are the mouth of ch'i) are best located on the wall directly opposite the bed or on the walls on either side, but only if they are near the corner farthest from the bed. The upper part of the bed should remain protected.

To place a door on a side wall where it is even with the bed would mean that the door, the mouth of ch'i, would blast the sleeper with a broadside of energy that would likely disturb sleep. However, the worst place for a door would be in the wall behind the headboard. This is the symbolic north, and ch'i from this direction is the worst kind. Energy should not flow into a room from behind the sleeper since he would be vulnerable to unexpected intrusions.

In this beach house the bed is placed so that the door is in the same wall as the headboard–the worst possible position. However, that it is a beach house must be taken into consideration. Any room open to the ocean receives its primary ch'i from that direction, no matter whether through a door or a window, thus giving this particular room an excellent feng shui configuration. Upon entering, we face the fame wall, which is in the direction of the ocean, the most important of all factors in a beach house. But more important, the primary entry of ch'i into the room is from the same direction, which renders the door only a secondary entrance for ch'i, on a level, say, with a window. A window in the unprotected north wall is not ideal, but it is less problematic than a doorway.

The huge oil painting at the head of the bed dominating the area seemed to be of pale figures with hands linked. Around this painting were placed striking photographs of chimpanzees. "The painting always impressed me as being a part of a circle," the owner said. "You notice the way you could be looking up from within this circle . . . taking part in it yourself."

The circle, I said, is an appropriate shape for the bedroom. It connotes love, compassion, completeness, and equality.

"Yes," he agreed. "And the photographs of the chimpanzees are really, kind of, almost shocking. But they indicate the closeness between man and primates in the real sense of the word 'animal.' I don't think that chain should be broken." ■

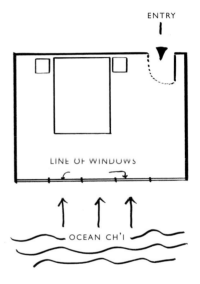

In beach houses, those rooms open to the ocean admit so much energy that the "ocean side" becomes the primary entrance of ch'i, thus creating an alternative "correct" position for the bed, as displayed in this master bedroom. A doorway from behind is permitted because its flow of energy is secondary to the energy off the ocean. The door thus takes on a subordinate role in the admission of ch'i into the room.

THE WRIGHT HOUSE

This is a Frank Lloyd Wright house. It is also a house with a curious twist. For some reason Wright thought that Sol Friedman, the original owner, was a toy manufacturer, and during construction from 1949 to 1950, he good-naturedly referred to the site as "Toy Hill." Later, in an architectural magazine he spoke fondly of "the house for the toy makers," referring to the whole family. Friedman was, in fact, a retailer, but Wright's misconception gave the house an indelible stamp of humor and whimsy.

Approaching the site via the forested drive, you can see the round outlines of the main house, the carport, and the terrace sprouting from the hillside like a cluster of mushrooms. Making the last

OPPOSITE Frank Lloyd Wright achieved an extraordinary balance of yin and yang through the design placement and the building materials utilized in this round-shaped house.

BELOW Wright's plan of the site on Toy Hill.

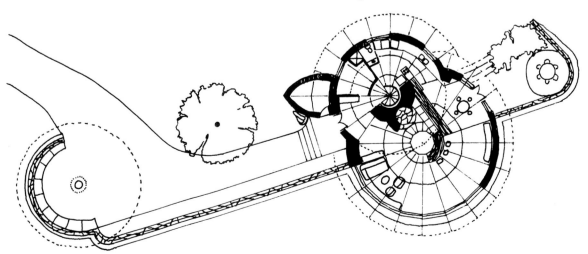

Standing at the foot of the retaining walls of the carport, the walkway, and the house, one has the impression of a miniature castle.

Michael's favorite place to view his house is from a sitting area beneath the carport. The open expanse of lawn (yang) contrasts agreeably with the canopied yin of the wooded area.

turn, you discover an open, circular carport supported by a single central column—quite like a mushroom. By the time you park beneath this fanciful structure, your imagination is working overtime, and you are the elfin toy maker returning home after a hard day in Santa's workshop.

Michael and Maria Osheowitz are the third owners since the house was built. They have preserved the site with few changes, adapting their family to Wright's formidable and sometimes imposing vision. Over the years, however, they have noticed aspects of the house that they felt could benefit from a fresh approach. The challenge for me, as both a feng shui consultant and an architect, was to bring to this unique house suggestions that would be consistent with Wright's original conception. Wright himself recognized that houses normally have a succession of owners, and that any design has to be adapted to changing needs and circumstances.

I have found no evidence that Wright had any knowledge of feng shui, though his views closely paralleled much of what I have come to admire and appreciate in this ancient discipline. However, Wright did live in the Far East for a while, during the construction of the Imperial Hotel in Tokyo, one of his most celebrated buildings. It is possible that he was introduced to feng shui at that time, but by then he was already a mature architect with his own fully developed style. On a practical level Wright showed little concern for some feng shui details, like knife edges, as we will see in this house. Still his work, in the main, follows feng shui principles more closely than that of any other major contemporary architect.

I began the consultation with Michael and Maria with a discussion of the exterior, which seemed a bit cold because of all the stonework. My recommendation was a fountain to soften the entrance and make it more welcoming. Wright himself designed fountains in other homes of this type using only copper tubing from which water fell into natural-looking stone basins. From a feng shui point of view, water is the element associated with the career side of the ba-gua (the career side being the side of the main entrance), and so a fountain was doubly appropriate.

Inside, the first problem that concerned me was a knife edge—floor to ceiling in stone—that greeted each person as they entered the house. This was a difficult problem to address because, typical of

Beneath the whimsical carport, which literalizes the mushroom motif, you might imagine yourself to be an elfin toy maker.

To soften the exterior, a small fountain based on the fountain at Fallingwater was added next to the front door. The photograph was taken on the day of the installation, so the ivy had not had time to conform to the contours of the stones.

A plant and a sinuous carved walking stick have been positioned against the stone to soften a knife edge just inside the entrance. Ivy trained to grow on the wall would be the best long-term solution. The negative effect of the spiral staircase is ameliorated by a skylight on the second floor that brings in light and positive energy.

Wright entryways, there was not a lot of room for a corrective device. This was also a well-trafficked area, and anything that protruded into the hall could be more disruptive than the knife edge itself. I suggested mounting something narrow on the wall to distract the eye from the knife edge. We decided on a sculpted walking stick and a plant placed to one side. In feng shui the play of one element off another (called "balancing the elements") is a common device for affecting change. The sinuous wood of the walking stick was only a temporary corrective measure. Eventually, something larger and flatter, like ivy, would be better, particularly if it could be trained to grow on the stone.

The entrance had another potential problem that, interestingly, had already been solved by Wright. In feng shui spiral staircases are thought to be dangerous because they "bore" into the floors like a corkscrew. Possibly this idea arose because people are more likely to trip on spiral staircases than standard stairs, particularly if the stairs are made of dark material or not well lit. Also, the middle of the home is thought to be a poor place for such a stairway because of its implications for health (the center position being the position for self and health). Wright thoughtfully energized the area by placing a skylight above the staircase that provides natural light at least during the day.

Entering the living room, we experienced one of Wright's favorite devices, the opening of a small foyer into an expansive living space. Wright used this technique to give even the smallest homes the feeling of comfortable accommodation. In feng shui it is an example of juxtaposing yin and yang elements to achieve a desired effect.

Along the curved wall of the living room unusual reverse Palladian windows with a curve at their base instead of at the top look out onto a wooded area to the south. In feng shui the upright Palladian window is thought to have negative connotations, as it resembles a tombstone, while the reverse form is considered beneficial because the rounded bottoms are thought to hold your luck like a bowl. At the least, one can say that Wright avoided the institutional or monastery look of Palladian windows by inverting them.

The reverse Palladian windows with their scooped-out bottoms are thought to retain good luck. The view, into the upper part of the forest canopy, gives the feeling of being high in the trees.

The concrete floor in the living room displays a radiating line pattern suggestive of a cobweb or perhaps heat from the hearth. In fact, the pipes of the original heating system are still embedded in the concrete. The system gave out some years ago, and to repair it would have meant tearing up the floor to replace the piping. Michael and Maria decided that that would be too disruptive and instead added a new heating system with small radiators screened with covers copied from a design that Wright used in Taliesin, his house and school in Wisconsin.

A large fireplace occupies the center of the house. Its chimney rises through the center of the second floor to serve as the core around which all the rooms on both floors are clustered. The suggestion is of a great tree with the hearth and chimney as the trunk.

Wood and earth are definitely the elements that rule this home, with earth, represented by stone and concrete, being the more predominant. In the initial design wood played an even greater role. Long oak beams fanned out from the central chimney like limbs of a tree. But Wright made an interesting decision. When he walked into the house during construction, he looked up at the beams and found them "too busy," and so another layer of ceiling plaster was added to conceal them, thus tipping the balance in favor of stone.

Still, something of the feeling of a tree remains. When one looks out the reverse Palladian windows into the wooded area—on a lower level than the house—one has a sense of being in a forest

OPPOSITE **The round shape of the balcony and the concrete dining table seems to extend the protection of the hearth to those who sit at the table.**

The dining area, on the fame side, echoes the mushroom motif. Adjacent to a curved glass wall, it seems to place diners outdoors no matter what the weather.

According to Chinese folklore, a mirror behind the stove doubles the burners, doubles the food, and doubles prosperity. (In Chinese the words for *wealth* and *food* sound the same.) It also lightens the area and gives the cook a view of the rest of the room.

canopy. Also, the heavy wood of the balcony suspended over the fireplace looks a bit like the walls of a treehouse in high branches.

Continuing around the curve of the room, we come to a dining area just inside an outdoor terrace. The little round wooden stools, also of Wright's design, look like tiny mushrooms sprouting around a central mushroom, the round dining table. This area and the kitchen are located along the fame side of the ba-gua, which indicates the value placed by the couple on the nurturing of friends and family.

Almost completing our circle around the central fireplace, we come to the kitchen, where the stove is placed on the inside wall. Unfortunately, it *faces* the wall so the view is blocked, making the cooking area a bit dark and unwelcoming. I proposed the addition of a large mirror behind the stove to visually open up the area and, of course, to satisfy the feng shui requirement of giving the cook some view or perspective of the rest of the room. Mirrors behind stoves are also thought to enhance prosperity, as they symbolically double the food being prepared.

Up the spiral staircase we come to a small balcony, a kind of mezzanine overlooking the living room. Originally the playroom for the children of the "toy maker," it is almost a real treehouse. The Osheowitzes' children, too, played here, but now that they are grown the area has become a library. It still has the feel of a treehouse, however, with the exposed beams of wood more in evidence here than in the living room. While such an enclosed, yin area is appropriate for children, it is a bit restrictive for adults, perhaps because of its low

ceiling. The solution was to cover the end wall, above the banquette, with a full mirror so that not only does the space seem to be expanded but the beams and reverse oval pattern of the windows, characteristic of this space, are nicely echoed.

The bedrooms are on the top floor; they are roughly pie-shaped, with a curved outer wall that, again, makes it seem as if one is living around the trunk of a tree. Their small size, built-in fixtures, and clean woodwork give them a feeling of ship- or cabinlike effi-

A balcony overlooking the living room felt too constricted for adults. A mirror on the far wall above the banquette enlarges the space. The low ceiling, however, preserves the yin quality of the former playroom, now used as a library. Note the knife edge corner softened by pillows.

ABOVE **Earth, in the form of concrete and stone, is dominant throughout most of the home. In the upstairs bedrooms, however, wood prevails. Wright's clean, simple lines and proportions promote a feeling of order and harmony.**

ABOVE RIGHT **A high window in the bedroom allows privacy but grants a view of trees during the day. Large windows in a small room such as this could destroy the sense of privacy and the yin security of the room. The bilateral symmetry of the lamp/fan at the head of the bed is a metaphor for "couple."**

ciency. For space reasons the beds could not be square without intruding too much into the irregularly shaped rooms. Wright's solution was to have the beds built as pie-shaped wedges. This always elicits questions from visitors, but having the foot of the bed narrower than the head has never been a problem for the Osheowitzes since, as they explained, there is less "body" to spread out at that end. Sheets are expensive, of course, since they must be custom-made, but the beds are a symbol of their home's uniqueness: one of the small prices to pay for living within a work of art.

The built-in fixtures in the upstairs rooms are all made of natural wood. Efficient, with clean lines, they promote a sense of order and encourage restful sleep. One senses the shift to wood in the upstairs rooms where concrete, much in evidence downstairs, has almost disappeared. Rush baskets add to the feeling of wholeness with nature and a oneness with earth.

The core of the second floor is the stairwell and central chimney around which the bedrooms and bath are clustered. The center position of the house is important in the defining of self, as well as for its association with health. Accessed by the spiral stairway and lighted by the skylight, the area could still run the risk of seeming small and cramped. At my suggestion a small-faceted crystal was suspended from the ceiling to catch the sun's rays and add life and depth. On the central wall surrounding the chimney the Osheowitzes placed brightly colored Mexican masks. "They were used for dances," explained Maria. "Some of them are devils. Some of them are very whimsical, more playful than frightening."

"The pink faces are depicting conquistadores," added Michael. "So these are really Maria's heritage: the two Spaniards over there, and the Indian god over here." In their variety they also represented the facets of human experience, from the whimsical and joyful to the dark, all of which must be acknowledged, lived with, and kept in balance in the harmonious home.

It was interesting that Michael and Maria placed the masks in the center of the house. Perhaps it was a way of marking this distinctive space as theirs. Sometimes, living in an important or historical home, one can feel more like a tenant or a guest than an owner. Wright did not want his houses to overpower their occupants; still, you cannot live in such a place unmindful of its creator. To be happy there, you must acknowledge its past and . . . for the present, make it your own. ∎

The upstairs hallway and staircase are enlivened by skylights and a crystal that distributes energy in its spangled refractions. The dance masks represent various aspects of the psyche to be acknowledged and balanced in the harmonious home.

American Master Drawings and Water[e]

Works on Paper from Colonial Times to the P[r]
Whitney Museum of American Art
November 23, 1976–January 23, 1977

JAPONISME

12

JAPANESE BLOSSOMS, AMERICAN ROOTS

Sometimes, there are very few, if any, changes resulting from a feng shui consultation. If a space has been constructed correctly, and the objects within it arranged in a meaningful manner, then I may be content simply to hear the reasons why and to exchange ideas on placement and intention. I began to suspect this was going to be the case when I entered Laurie Kerr's Greenwich Village loft. Laurie is an architect; her partner is an editor and a collector of American art.

In the entry foyer, just inside the front door, the proportions are simple. The art, which has been placed with great care, is all Americana. On the family wall to the right, a woman in a Winslow Homer print reclines in the grass and reads. To the left of the door, an eighteenth-century woman gazes across the parquet floor to an antique boat becalmed on the "fame" wall painted an aqua blue. Laurie's father, I later learned, was a captain in the navy. Her grand-father was an admiral.

According to the ba-gua, water is the element associated with the career side of a space, the side on which the main entry is located. Laurie's placement of the boat and the selection of the aqua color were, of course, suggestive of water. Even the parquet floor of maple

OPPOSITE Open areas of the foyer are broken into pleasing proportions by maple woodwork that seems to exemplify Japanese shoji screens and modernized Shaker style. The parquet echoes patterns from American patchwork quilts.

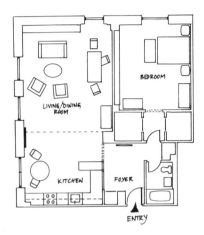

ABOVE **Floor plan of Laurie Kerr's loft.**

RIGHT **A kimono spreads its arms above an American hobbyhorse. These two symbols of the couple's interests are brought together on the fame wall (when viewed from the perspective of the room) and the family wall (when viewed from the perspective of the entire apartment).**

and cherry seemed to orient one like a nautical compass (although it also seemed to evoke the pattern of a patchwork quilt). Around me clean lines of latticelike woodwork broke up both wall and open space, providing perches for objects such as old-fashioned egg scales along the top shelf or weathered decoy birds. However, another influence was at work here, too, something I couldn't quite put my finger on, but which contributed to the good craftsmanship and simple lines.

A turn into the main living space revealed the other influence. A Japanese kimono hung on the wall in crucifix form above an American hobbyhorse. "During my childhood," Laurie said, "I lived in Japan for two years. My brother still does. I am greatly influenced by the Japanese preference for clean, simple lines, and their focus on the quality and beauty of the materials. Early American design shares these attributes, making for a natural consonance between them. The maple framework in the foyer, for instance, is a kind of modernized Shaker design with a Japanese twist." It had been installed, she told me, by a marine carpenter.

The kimono, which hangs on the "fame" wall (when viewing the room from the foyer doorway), is unusual in design. A patchwork "under" kimono, it is sewn together from bits and pieces of older kimonos and worn beneath the more elaborate outer garment. "It's the same idea as the American patchwork quilt," Laurie explains, "just realized in a different context." The wooden hobbyhorse below, missing its tail, is late nineteenth century, probably carved for a child by his father.

The juxtaposition of these two objects was quite satisfying, for several interesting reasons. The ba-gua, when oriented to the entire apartment (that is, using the front door for orientation), shows the wall with the kimono and horse to be on the family side. However, considering the room by itself, the same wall is on the fame side. Thus, fame and family are combined in one wall, with both people bringing to it objects representing their strongest personal interests:

Evoking the tradition of the American patchwork quilt, the "under" kimono is perfectly at home stretched above the quintessential American folk toy, the hobbyhorse.

A seating area in or near the wealth and power corner is an indication of the value placed upon friends. With this arrangement Laurie welcomes her friends to share and appreciate her loft and the many objects of art she and her partner have collected.

Laurie, her Japanese collection, and her partner, an Americana collection. Their interests (fame) are melded in their relationship (family).

During renovation, several years ago, the room in which we stood was discovered to have a vaulted ceiling: a welcome surprise. "It's very light," said Laurie, "and reminds me of clouds." At the far end of the room two strong areas contrast agreeably, the wealth and power corner and the marriage/relationship corner. The seating area, in the wealth and power corner on the left, is an active yang area. The shelves contain books of her partner, many of which she edited. The head of a lion from a copper cornice guards the library.

The seating area in front of the library also falls within the wealth and power corner. Here their wealth is in their friends, who are made welcome by this placement of couch and leather chairs. The prominent location of the seating area, and the obvious care of the furnishings, sends a signal to visitors that they are both welcome and important in the lives of the two women who live here.

The dining area to the right is sparse and serene, a pleasant yin space that contrasts with the yang energy of the opposite wealth and power corner. The large Japanese screen, mounted on the wall, belonged to Laurie's maternal grandmother. According to the bagua, we are in the marriage/relationship corner, also known as the mother side, which is an appropriate location for a beautiful feminine heirloom. The screen itself depicts two birds on a snowy bough, a symbol of relationship.

The table beneath the screen began as a design project that Laurie took on, "to make something beautiful out of simple plywood." From an inexpensive material that is easily at hand and that has definite characteristics, she created a table in a stripped-down deco style reminiscent of that of the German designer Jacques-Emile Ruhlmann. The chairs at either end are originals by Hans Wagner, a 1940s designer, and are of a perfect weight so as not to overpower the table. The smaller chair, behind the table, is a nineteenth-century piece made of violin wood. Hanging above is a wrought-iron chandelier that is French turn-of-the-century. The strength of this eclectic grouping is in the harmony achieved despite the diversity of the var-

The dining area is dominated by a Japanese screen depicting two birds on a snowy bough. An heirloom from Laurie's maternal grandmother, the scroll is appropriately placed in the marriage/relationship corner, which is also identified with the mother. The table, built by Laurie, supports the gentle, yin images above.

Empowered by its position in the marriage/relationship corner, an early American quilt symbolizes the yin qualities of patience, hard work, and nurturing. The Tansu chest is another heirloom from Laurie's maternal grandmother.

OPPOSITE Placing objects at comfortable eye level is part of tailoring a space for its occupants. The art gallery for Annie, Laurie's longhaired dachshund, is seen close to the floor to the left of the door. Currently on display are a Keith Haring, a Jean-Honoré Fragonard, and an anonymous piece of American folk art, all, unfortunately, reproductions.

ious components. Personal commitment is reflected here, as are sensitivity and a striving for balance.

The bedroom is located in the marriage/commitment corner . . . always appropriate for enhancing a relationship. Upon entering, I noticed first an American patchwork quilt displaying the pinecone pattern. In its simple geometry, form and function were perfectly wedded, exemplifying the classical, Western approach to art and interior design. A Japanese Tansu chest from Laurie's maternal grandmother was at the foot of the bed, reflecting the same values.

Humor in an apartment or home speaks volumes about the people who live there. I noticed a carved wooden panel of birds mounted slightly too high above the bed and asked Laurie why. "Bird's-eye level," she quipped with a smile, and I could not object. "Actually, it's a transom panel salvaged from a Japanese house" (perhaps another reason for its being mounted so high). "It's got two birds on a branch, the theme from the scroll in the dining room.

"And now, turn around," she said mischievously.

Above, on a maple beam, was a bird, perhaps a raven, perched above her bedroom door. But it was not the wooden bird to which she referred, it was three small paintings of dogs, postcard-size, mounted near the floor. I knew what they were at once—and laughed.

"That's Annie's picture gallery," Laurie said. Annie is their longhaired dachshund. "Annie's taste is very eclectic. She has a Keith Haring, a Fragonard, and a piece of American folk art." In feng shui terms we were in the children/creative side of the apartment.

A collection of pottery and glassware extends across the career wall. The aluminum pot on the stove provides a reflective surface, a cure for the cook to view the rest of the room.

For our last stop, we returned to the main room and focused on the kitchen area. Shelves extending across the entire wall bore another grouping of Japanese/American crafts: American yellowware and brownware bowls and a variety of Japanese ceramics. Below, the stove was mounted against the wall. This was one of the few problems I had seen in the apartment; a correction was needed, such as a wind chime, to warn of an entry into the room while the cook's back was turned. Since Laurie didn't like wind chimes, I mentioned that in traditional Chinese families, a polished wok was often used for the same purpose. Hung on the wall behind the stove, it would provide a serviceable convex mirror. We compromised on a large polished aluminum pot, which now sits permanently on top of the stove.

The simple breakfast table beneath the window allowed for an excellent view of the river. One does not see the Hudson without feeling a sense of its calming power. As we sat there we discussed feng shui and the various meanings displayed in their apartment. "Most of the American objects are my partner's," Laurie said. "The Japanese things are mine. As an architect my goal was to give them both a home."

This was an interesting and, I believe, correct approach. Objects, whether works of art or simple kitchen utensils, carry unique meaning and memory for each of us, which is as it should be. These objects are simply markers that trigger our conscious or subconscious minds. With the help of these objects—and our space—we can become more in touch with ourselves, more focused, more loving, more confident, and more at peace.

The influence of objects can be simple and direct, such as a photograph on our desk that reminds us of why we are working so hard, or a trophy won in a sports competition that reminds us of our skills, or perhaps a tree we planted in the yard that reminds us of a departed relative or friend. I view it as the job of feng shui to help us understand and utilize the energy of those associations.

Laurie explained her own approach to feng shui: "Much of what I see in contemporary Western art is based on geometry, more mathematically driven than symbolic. My own architecture reflects this Western formalism but feng shui provides for another layer of association and inventiveness. Perhaps it is the key to what can be done on a small scale. It provides a framework where I had never thought to make decisions before." ∎

Architectural miniatures are ideal souvenirs for an architect, and are well placed in the travel corner. Reminders with pleasant associations can be a source of positive energy.

A PLACE TO REST

S ig Bergamin isn't home a lot. A designer with an international
clientele, he divides his time between the United States, Brazil,
and other countries where he has ongoing projects. Not surprisingly,
he has trouble getting a full night's sleep. People who travel frequently, or divide their time between more than one home, often
need places of rest that are more protective and supportive than
usual, for they must convince their subconscious, wherever they are,
that they are, indeed, in a safe and nurturing place.

Sig was intrigued by feng shui and curious about how it might
relate to his own approach to interior design. When I came to see
him, he did not realize the level of personal introspection that a consultation involves. What I learned about Sig was that even though his
house was beautifully decorated, comfortable, and welcoming to his
friends, he himself did not have a place to rest.

When I drove to the site, the first thing I noticed was the
entrance to the front garden. The rounded overhead trellis and the
scooped-out gate below combined to form a circle, resembling the
traditional Chinese "moon gate." Used as a symbol of welcome and
good fortune, these gates always create a feeling of gracious accommodation. This is partly because yin shapes are more welcoming

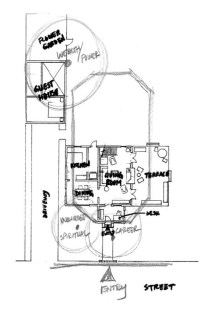

The ba-gua placed over the entire
property.

OPPOSITE **This circular arbor echoes
the welcoming curve of the Chinese
"moon gate." Alignment with the
front door is beneficial as long as ch'i
does not escape quickly from the
house. Foliage slows the departing
ch'i nicely.**

than yang. (Yang shapes tend to challenge.) Also, I noticed that the gate was exactly aligned with the doorway of the house, another good aspect of the design. There would be no momentary confusion about which way to go, which door to enter.

There is a danger, however, to aligning an outdoor gate with the entrance to a home. If the path joining the two is straight and unobstructed, then energy may move too quickly, both to and from the house, carrying with it perhaps luck, and even fortune. But here again, Sig had unconsciously done the right thing. The gate has swinging doors, which slow the passage of ch'i. Also, plants surrounding and overhanging the arch soften one's overall impression of the entrance and further slow the ch'i.

The front walk, the lawn and gardens, and the front door are well maintained. In Sig's case that is particularly important because he works out of his home. According to the ba-gua, the entry is on the career side, and, practically speaking, it is the first thing that a potential client sees. If you work out of your home, judgments may be made that affect your business before you even hear your doorbell ring.

Sig greeted me at the door, and the next thing I took note of was his desk. He had placed it in the entry foyer just inside the front door. Unfortunately, it faced a side window, a location that was problematic in two ways. First, he was looking out a window that did not give a view of people approaching the house. In fact, his back was to the front door. Second, the window he faced was covered with pho-

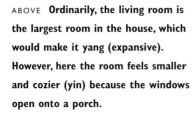

ABOVE **Ordinarily, the living room is the largest room in the house, which would make it yang (expansive). However, here the room feels smaller and cozier (yin) because the windows open onto a porch.**

ABOVE RIGHT **The oversize hearth, always a yin symbol, is in the center of the future/creativity wall. The marriage/relationship corner (in the far center of the photo) had contained an arrangement of dried flowers. The negative energy of dead plants was unfortunate in the context of the abundant life in Sig's garden.**

tos and postcards that almost obliterated what view there was. As important as photos and mementos are, they should not become an impediment or a distraction from work. In Sig's case, symbols of family and friends, correctly positioned, could help reinforce his sense of home and belonging. The problem was balancing their influence with his professional life.

I asked him how he felt about the desk. "Oh, I love sitting here," he said. "I could talk on the phone all day here, but I don't get much work done." His answer did not surprise me, but there was an immediate and simple solution. I proposed that the desk be turned so that he looked out the front window, which was unobstructed. In this position the approach of visitors or clients was directly in his line of vision. Friends and family were still present in the window where their pictures were placed, but they were to the side and would distract him less.

Otherwise, the arrangement in the entry foyer was good. Even though the space was quite small it was energized by a skylight so that Sig did not feel hemmed in at the desk. In fact, during the day the light made the small foyer seem even more expansive than the adjacent living room, which was quite a bit larger.

We next entered the living room, and I immediately sensed the enclosed, yin feeling of the space. It was appropriate for an intimate seating arrangement promoting harmony among family and friends. It was also an excellent place to "talk shop," as the room was on the creativity side of the house. A wide variety of shapes and textures gave the room an eclectic feeling. In the marriage/relationship corner, however, I noticed a small wooden corner piece with shells and dried flowers on the shelves. Empty shells are not the most positive objects one could place in this important area, and dried flowers are about the worst. I suggested a round corner table, round being the most appropriate shape for the relationship corner. Then I encouraged him to enliven the area with cut flowers from his garden whenever possible. And last, Sig chose from his many knickknacks a dancing couple in porcelain to perch atop the table.

French doors in the living room look out onto an outdoor terrace. As the focal point from the marriage/relationship corner, the view needed to be warm and inviting. The two white chairs and round table were appropriate, but without the tree they would have

The canopy of the tree is crucial in creating this comfortable sitting area. Because it is in the marriage/relationship corner, additional enclosure, such as hedges, walls, or plants, is advisable.

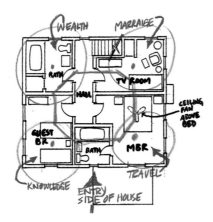

Second floor, existing layout.

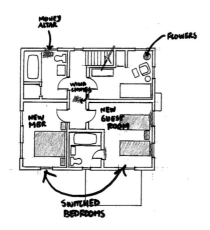

Second floor, proposed layout.

been entirely too barren. I suggested that shrubs or perhaps a low wall should be added before next summer to make the area less exposed and give it more of a protected, sheltered feeling.

Going upstairs, we entered the hallway that runs the length of the second story. I mentioned to Sig that in feng shui the end of a hallway is a special place where a great deal of energy is channeled simply by virtue of the parallel walls. There must always be something special at the end to receive that energy; otherwise, the viewer sees the end of the hall as a barrier or an obstruction. In Sig's case this spot was doubly important because it was on the career wall of the house. What I saw was near perfection. Sig had turned this area of significance into a floor-to-ceiling display cabinet for his favorite glass pieces. Even the colors were perfect, mostly reds, which stand for fame, and yellows, which represent the self. More than a simple collection, the display was also an extension of his career. Sig told me that he loved to go antiquing and is well known for his expeditions to Connecticut and upstate New York. In fact, journalists have written about his trips to rural antiques stores for period pieces, Americana, and just plain kitsch.

On the second floor the master bedroom is located in the travel corner, a bad location given Sig's lifestyle. In addition, the bed was improperly placed. The door of the room entered directly onto the side of the bed, making for an excess of energy "broadsiding" the sleeper and disturbing his rest. To top it off, a ceiling fan hung right above the bed. Ceiling fans circulate ch'i as well as air, and both

LEFT **A number of things conspired to make Sig's bedroom unworkable. It was in the travel corner; the bed could not be properly positioned; and the fan was directly above the bed.**

ABOVE **A hallway channels its energy to the end of the corridor. In Sig's house the second-floor hallway goes from the back of the house to the front, so the corridor's fame wall is the career wall for the entire structure. Sig displays there part of his glass collection.**

swirling about him could be disruptive to rest. I asked Sig how he liked the bedroom. He said that he seldom used it, preferring usually to sleep in the adjacent TV room. I could see why.

Because of the size of the master bedroom and the placement of doors and windows, there was really no ideal rearrangement possible. I suggested instead that he switch the master bedroom with the guest room across the hall. He was delighted with the idea. Before leaving the former master bedroom, I suggested adding a mosquito netting canopy to give guests the option of cutting down on some of the energy of the circulating fan. Sig said he would move the twin beds into the room, which will take guests directly out from under the swirling blades.

Sig is most comfortable in the TV room located in the marriage/relationship corner. Although there is space for only a twin bed, a stuffed chair will create comfortable lounging for two. Paintings mounted in pairs, two pillows with fish, and two vases symbolize couples.

Next, we went to see the TV room, one of Sig's favorite spaces to unwind, watch TV, or simply nap. It was in the marriage/relationship corner, which meant it had overtones of nurturing and protection, certainly more in line with Sig's needs than the travel corner. Since he was still using it as a temporary bedroom, we added items in pairs, including two pillows with embroidered fish and two

vases for the side table. There was only room for one twin-size bed and so an additional reading chair was added to create a lounging area for two.

The bathroom on the second floor is in the wealth and power corner, not the best location; if not corrected, it means that money is being flushed away. We decided on the color red as a cure. In feng shui it is a color of good fortune. Sig was uncomfortable with painting the entire room red so we introduced the color selectively. First, from his collection of kitsch we found an old brakeman's lantern and placed it in the window. Next a red bowl was filled with rice, a symbol of prosperity, and nine red envelopes containing money were placed in it. Both of these boldly colored items were striking reminders to Sig to manage his money more carefully.

A bathroom in the wealth and power corner needs correction to prevent a drain on luck and money. In the West, the color red, which has among its connotations "stop," can be used as a cure. Here it is introduced with accent pieces, the red brakeman's lantern and the red rice bowl with red envelopes containing money.

THE COTTAGE

In a corner of his property is a lovely cottage made particularly inviting by the lush gardens, trellised vines, and potted plants. Sig said that in the summer he loved bringing in fresh flowers. In feng shui flowers are one of the ultimate symbols of good luck.

Placing the ba-gua on the cottage, I found the doorway to be in the helpful people corner. Thus the flowers and the care he has taken with the entrance to the cottage take on an additional significance. His friends—the helpful people in his life—are welcomed with this positive energy.

When we stepped inside the cottage, Sig admitted that the

Sig rests better and is more in control of the entire site from this small cottage in the wealth and power corner. When orienting the ba-gua to the cottage, we find the entrance is in the helpful people and travel corner. Abundant flowers and plants symbolize Sig's good fortune in having many friends.

OPPOSITE The loft bed is on the family side, a position of rest and nurturing. The travel corner (where the camera is positioned) is taken up by the door, which swings inward. In effect, the travel corner is used to the point of nonexistence—exactly what Sig needs in a place of rest.

sleeping loft of this little one-room structure was the one place on all his property where he felt most secure. When guests came, he often gave them the big house so that he could have this beautiful space to himself. His declaration made sense from a feng shui perspective, for the cottage, considering the entire site, was actually positioned in the wealth and power corner. From there he had a view of all his domain: the house and the gardens. In the sleeping loft, above the fame wall of the cottage, he could see the entire room below and the flower garden on the helpful people side. The ceiling fan, in the middle of the room, circulated fresh air but did not disturb the loft. Sig was in control here, surrounded by the flowers he loved and the col-

ABOVE The wealth and power corner of this little cottage reveals the source of Sig's inspiration. The abundant energy of flowers has been integrated into the fabrics, colors, and artwork of his designs for spaces all over the world.

RIGHT In this little room there seem to be flowers even where there aren't any. The colors of the throw pillows, draperies, lamp shade, and even book covers bring the energy of the garden into the cottage.

lections from his antiquing trips. The colorful objects he had chosen for this space—pillows, lamp shades, and prints—bright, eclectic, and full of life, seemed to bring the energy of the garden into the room itself. It was as if he were living in his garden and at the same time working at his office in the wealth and power corner—but his office was full of flowers.

As I was leaving, Sig showed me a memorial to a friend that he had placed in the front yard. This is something seldom done today. Unlike the ancient Chinese, we neither bury our dead on our own property nor have much control over the specifics of a burial location. In early feng shui, an entire branch of the discipline pertained to the propitious location of grave sites so that energy from the ancestors could reflect back on and enhance the lives of their descendants. On a piece of granite Sig had inscribed a single word: "believe." It was placed in front of the tree so that its message beamed back toward the house, much in the way the ancient graves projected the good ch'i of the ancestors back onto the living. If it were a real grave it would have been too close to the house and would have required backing (roughly shaped like a horseshoe) to collect and channel the energies. However, I found no fault with this simple memorial, or reminder. The placement, in the knowledge and spirituality corner, was correct. ∎

In the knowledge and spirituality corner, a tree has been planted in memory of a friend.

G A R D E N   F E N G   S H U I

Our subject is the garden of a turn-of-the-century frame house in historic Alexandria, Virginia. I am accompanied by Lila Fendrick, the landscape architect who designed it. She explains that the owners, Washington executives, have asked to remain anonymous. Secrets are a part of the Washington landscape, but they have an important place in gardens, too. In fact, I tell Lila, every garden should have one.

The site is triangular overall; the house is at the wide end, and the garden in the "point" between two streets. In feng shui any structures, including streets, that form angles sharper than ninety degrees create strong paths of energy traditionally known as "poison arrows." Not all strong paths of energy need be negative. Still, the neighbors on the receiving end should take steps (if they know) to deflect any poison arrow aimed at their property. In this case, five streets have come together and there was no property directly across from the poison arrow to be harmed or to blast back with a poison arrow of its own.

Behind the arrow, the site can be harmed by the hasty draining of energy. At this site, it is important to note that the fences, one on either side of the garden, do not actually meet to literalize the point

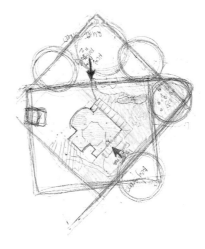

ABOVE **My working feng shui sketch, experimenting with ba-gua placement over the property.**

OPPOSITE **A reproduction of an ancient Quan Yin sculpture used as a focus for meditation is placed in the knowledge corner, traditionally associated with meditation.**

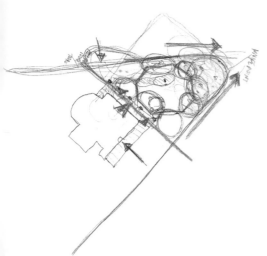

Site plan showing knife point.

The heavy plantings of trees, and the fact that fences on either side of the garden do not meet at the point where the streets cross, lessen the visual impact of the "poison arrow" and the potential drain of energy.

of the arrow, thereby slowing the flow of energy away from the site. In addition, the point has been heavily planted with trees, which mitigates the arrow effect somewhat while still maintaining the privacy screen. The trees chosen for this important spot are evergreens; therefore, the screen is in place all year round. The site retains its own ch'i, contributing little to the energy and conflict of the intersection beyond, an extremely diplomatic solution.

Still, it was not Lila's intention to cut the garden off from the outside world. She explained her objectives in the positioning of the two pools that form the heart of the garden: "By siting the upper pool on axis with the intersection, and the lower pool on axis with the French doors off the house, I was designing a continuous flow of energy along the longest axis of the garden. Locating the most animated elements (waterfall, pools) in this previously neglected and overlooked corner resulted in a change from negative to positive, from neglect to loving care, from dormancy to flowing energy."

The two fish ponds, terraced, with a waterfall between them, form the heart of the garden. The pleasant sound of falling water helps mask the noise from the street and enhances the sense of privacy. Water, because of its flat, calm surface, is an ideal mover of ch'i, but if there is little movement of the water itself, then it also becomes an ideal place for ch'i to collect. Thus water is considered to enhance prosperity.

One of the principles of the Chinese garden is that nothing should look man-made. A pool, for instance, should have a natural

shape, no sharp or square corners, as if it had been formed on that very spot. The stone for these pools was chosen for that effect. "It's called Pennsylvania Endless Mountain Stone," Lila explains. "These particular stones are from walls and streambeds and have nice rounded edges. Often they're covered with lichens and mosses."

Fish are symbols of abundance and prosperity, particularly goldfish because of their red and orange coloring. In traditional thinking they add a slight motion to the water, keeping the ch'i

A natural look is preferred in Chinese gardens, where there is no sign of the artifice of man. Soft grasses add to the feeling of being "nestled" in a safe retreat.

ABOVE **Fish and water are both symbols of abundance. In the center of the garden, they signify an abundance of health.**

RIGHT **In this shaded retreat, the uplifted forms of some plants contrast with the soft, retiring forms of others. Lighter and darker shades of green create a narrow but varied color palette, and dapples of sunlight in the afternoon add to this subtle mosaic of yin and yang.**

moving. A self-contained pool without these excellent fish could become stagnant and a breeding place for mosquitoes.

While it is clear that the pools are in the center of the garden space—which is the position of the self and of health—it is not clear how the other points of the garden are to be interpreted. The ba-gua can be oriented either from the property entrance or from the French doors that open onto the portico of the house. In deciding which is more appropriate, function is an excellent guide. When the owners enter the property, frequently after a long day at work, the house is usually their immediate goal. At such times they have a sense of the garden's presence, on the far left in the spirituality corner, but the house, straight ahead, is their destination, placing it on the fame wall. In this case the garden is sensed as a place of retreat, even if it is not immediately entered or used that way.

When the owners wish to use the garden, they usually enter it from the house. From this perspective (taking the front door as the mouth of ch'i), the garden occupies primarily the marriage/relationship corner and the future/children area; thus, there is a great emphasis on the right side of the ba-gua, which is the yin side. This garden is not about fame or career (yang attributes). Its function is to nurture (a yin attribute) and to provide sustenance for the future.

When entering the property from the street, one turns left to see the garden. A crepe myrtle tree tends to obscure the view, encouraging a closer look. In the afternoon, sunlight will also enter from behind to highlight the variety of textures and colors. The trees and house are arranged so that they receive maximum sunlight late in the day. This is an afternoon garden. It has also been carefully designed for low maintenance. Lila explains: "The point of this garden is not about bloom. It's all about green volumes, textures, and massing." For this reason plants were carefully chosen to provide a wide variety of shades and contrasting shapes and sizes. In the summer the garden feels so abundant that it comes as a surprise to realize that there are no blooms.

Entering from the street, one cannot see the entire garden at once. The curve of the stone walk and the screen of the crepe myrtle seem to invite us to come closer.

The straight lines of the porch contrast agreeably with the curvilinear shapes of the natural landscape. In this case the outdoors seems more yin than the enclosure of the house.

Turning to look back at the street, we see one of the well-proportioned wooden fences built to screen that segment of the garden from the street. One of the functions of a garden is to provide a feeling of privacy outdoors, which is hard to do if the eye is not kept within the site or if sounds from the street intrude. Here, a subtle combination of fence, shrubs, trees, and elevation keeps our focus within the garden without giving us a feeling of being restricted or confined.

At the house one is greeted by a portico with an open, slatted roof that gives the appearance of an arbor. From this perspective all of the garden is not visible. The straight lines of the porch, slatting,

The natural wood of the two fences that shield the garden harmonizes with the plants and rock. The open valence at the top avoids the impression of a hard enclosure.

An unused side door is made more welcoming by potted plants and a wind chime. If neglected, this area could harbor negative ch'i.

The little gargoyle emphasizes the aggressive energy of the pointed wall (poison arrow) on which it sits, discouraging use of this entrance.

and columns contrast agreeably with the natural curvilinear shapes of the landscape, especially the oval form of the pond. In this perspective, the roles of the house and garden are reversed. The house, although enclosed, has attributes of the yang: straight, hard lines. The garden, although more open (yang), seems soft and populated with rounded shapes (yin).

Traditionally, a garden has always embodied yin attributes, evoking a place of safety and retreat. The Chinese emphasize this yin perception by creating private, hidden places in their gardens. Probably it has been so since civilization began: the garden as refuge. Of course, we can only conjecture about earliest man, but it seems likely that in precivilized times the out-of-doors was something from which to escape. It was hard and full of danger while the cave or hut offered refuge. Civilized man has reversed that role: to escape *from* civilization with its pressures, we retreat to the garden.

The porch wraps around the house, and on its other side we find an unused entrance. Deserted spaces collect negative ch'i, and so a potted plant and a wind chime are added to enliven the area. Another contribution of the wind chime is symbolic security. On the same side of the house, a gate off the street is also not used because parking is no longer available there. A low wall just inside this entrance forms a poison arrow directed against any who would enter from that direction. In order to discourage use of this gate, we strengthen the poison arrow by placing on top of the low wall a statue of a gargoyle, the traditional warder of bad spirits.

LEFT **From the upper pond we detect no hint of a hideaway, only contrasts of shades, textures, and mass. A low-maintenance garden, it is at its best when only green.**

ABOVE **Following a trail of stepping-stones on the far side of the pond, we discover a secluded place, nearly hidden from the house. A colorful wind chime of natural agate marks the spot.**

The garden, however, has still not yielded its secret. Exploring further, we walk around the pond, where we find the beginning of a little path marked by round stepping-stones. Following it, we come to a tiny sitting area among the trees and shrubs that is almost completely hidden away. A well-placed rock invites us to sit for a while and survey the house and grounds. We have the feeling that if we sit perfectly still we will never be noticed by passersby. A light breeze stirs the leaves. The tinkle of a nearby wind chime keeps us company. ■

L I T T L E   S U R P R I S E S

Sometimes a building is so overpowering that it limits how much an individual can express himself or herself within its confines. Eliza Brook's apartment is in such a building. Her eighth-floor view of Gramercy Park comes with a manteled fireplace, herringbone parquet floors, substantial moldings, and a formal layout typical of upscale turn-of-the-century high-rises. It would have been enough to force most people into a comfortable conformity; however, Eliza has a sense of humor.

Upon entering her space, one is confronted by a floor-to-ceiling column that separates the living room on the left from the hallway on the right. I was concerned immediately that this column could be perceived as divisive, either to Eliza or her guests. It needed to be minimized by mounting on it an object of significance or one that reminded her of something important in her life. "Literature," she said, at once. "There are books on both sides of that wall, and they are central to my life." I proposed a solution that both represented her interests and did not intrude into the much-traveled passageway: to paint, actually illuminate, the front of the column with text from one of her favorite works. She suggested Chaucer's *Canterbury Tales,* a late-medieval collection of humorous and ribald

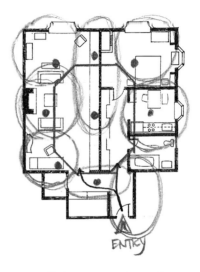

ABOVE **Circles representing my interpretation of the various areas of the ba-gua for this space.**

OPPOSITE **The column could be divisive or suggest obstructions. A calligraphic scroll was hung to soften the negative effects and to identify it more closely with the books on the wall behind it. Eventually, the column will be illuminated with passages from The Canterbury Tales.**

ABOVE **This unusual scene is a re-creation of a surrealist painting, *Time Transfixed* by René Magritte. The clock, bought expressly for the re-creation, doesn't run, so Eliza set it at her birthday.**

ABOVE RIGHT **As we enter the living room, we detect no signs of Eliza's whimsy. The bay window is on the fame wall and looks out onto Gramercy Park. The Phillipe Starck table/chair is in front of it. Sofas and chairs are gathered around the fire-place in the family area. Note the lamp on the "husband altar" beneath the two paintings.**

stories. In this way the column would be perceived as an affirmation of her love of literature and not as a divider of her space. Until an artist was found to execute the project, we agreed to hang on the column a simple black-and-white calligraphic scroll depicting an orchid and a Ming dynasty poem.

As I entered Eliza's living room, I noticed nothing unusual at first. The seating area, with sofas and chairs around the fireplace, forms a welcome spot to gather on the family side. A bay window with a banquette on the fame wall offers a much-sought-after view of the park. Impeccable furnishings include a Phillipe Starck chair (now in its closed position pretending to be an end table).

I suddenly noticed the fireplace, for out of its depths emerged

a model train on a golden trestle. "Does it work?" I asked, where-
upon I was treated to the headlights, the sound of its engine, and little puffs of smoke from its smoke stack. The fireplace, complete with
train, mantel, mirror, clock, and candlesticks, is a re-creation of a
painting titled *Time Transfixed* by René Magritte.

"The clock doesn't work," said Eliza. "When I bought it for the
arrangement I knew it would never run again, so I set it at my birth
date—but only the month and day," she added with a smile.

Part of her extensive library runs along one entire wall of the
living room, where intriguing whatnots, such as bronze men holding
up books, vie with more personal mementos. Among the miniature
prints a baby picture has been slipped in, unnoticed by two of her
grown stepdaughters (one of them the baby) for years. Other little
men, wooden artists' models, explore various parts of the room. Two
above the framed miniatures hold tiny spots that illuminate the
collection.

Wooden artists' models hold the
lighting fixtures for Eliza's art. They
seem to be contemporary parodies of
their traditional bronze counterparts
propping up books on the shelves.

"The room demanded a grown-up style," Eliza said, "unless I
was going to make it *really* a fun house—which I wasn't prepared to
do—so I decided on 'classical comfortable,' and it's not until you're
in the room—sitting down and looking around—that people say,
'Oh!'" Another example of her whimsy was in the hall. She showed
me how to pull back two bookshelves to reveal a secret closet—just
like in the movies.

Getting down to serious business, we considered next the location of her desk, and I saw an excellent example of an incorrect

OPPOSITE The "red dog" lamp marks
Eliza's desk, shown here in an incorrect placement made acceptable by
the proximity of the door and the
line of sight down the hall. The bookcase in the hall swings open to reveal
a hidden closet. The painting above
the desk is by Suzanne Geller.

From the kitchen one sees the wall
across the hall as part of the same
room. Eliza has arranged an exhibit
for the benefit of anyone sitting at
the table. The sphinx on the floor
guards her bedroom and helps to
make up for an incorrect placement
of the bed.

placement made right. Bearing a whimsical red dog lamp, the desk
was against the career wall. Although the wall was made more interesting by a contemporary painting, the desk faced squarely into it.
Yet the entrance of the room, immediately to the left, made it acceptable in feng shui terms. Without having to turn, anyone sitting at the
desk had a clear view of the entrance and an extensive view of the
hallway beyond. This location and orientation were thus an excellent alternative to the usual feng shui prescription, which in this case
would have included a mirror. Eliza's not being able to see what was
behind her might have been more important if there had been children in the apartment. As it was, her desk chair swiveled easily,
another accommodation to the rest of the room.

In the near bookcase I noticed photographs sitting on low
shelves, eye height for someone sitting down. "I don't like family pictures in everybody's face," Eliza said, gesturing from the desk, "so
these are just for me."

Eliza has a small, eat-in kitchen, typical of New York City. Red
walls energize the space but, as is the case for a small room, a view
through a window or door takes on an added degree of importance,
as it either provides needed perspective or becomes part of the room.
Here, the kitchen looks directly through the door onto the other side
of the book wall that divides the apartment. The impression is that
the wall across the hall actually becomes a dimension of the kitchen.
Utensils or kitchen-related art in this area could have visually
increased one's impression of the size of the room; however, Eliza

The bed is incorrectly placed since the door to the room is slightly behind it on the right. The sphinx outside the door is the cure.

The scroll, on the future side of the room, blocks an inauspicious view of another wing of the building and suggests new vistas. The orchid on the French bakery table adds life to the setting.

decided on a gallery approach. Art objects, paintings, prints, and miniature tea cups form a kind of display for anyone sitting at the kitchen table. It does not make the room seem larger but is visually quite pleasing.

The bedroom is in the marriage/relationship corner, always a good location for this important room. Eliza shared it with her husband until his death several years ago. Two large bay windows look out, one on the park and one toward another wing of the same building. The one with the less interesting view was hung with a beautiful stained-glass window purchased by her late husband. We discussed the events of her life since his death, and she indicated that she had come to a point in her life where she needed to move ahead on her own. If she was certain of this, I suggested, then there should be some symbol or marker of that decision. Perhaps she should move the stained-glass window that had hung in the same spot for so long to remind her that she had accepted his death and was ready to move on. The stained-glass window was taken down to be reset into the door of the bedroom. It would remain close, but its new position would transform it from a symbol of the past to one of the future, reinforcing her will to change.

Unfortunately, the view through the window, the corner of an adjacent wing of the building, did not please me. An ordinary corner, it was not sharp enough to be a poison arrow, and besides, it was not pointing at Eliza's window. Still, it was relatively close (denoting future obstructions), and it created a phenomenon known as "split

vision." When a vista is half blocked or a passage half obstructed, the eye is not sure where to focus and the next step is uncertain; one hesitates. This view was hardly appropriate for Eliza's future. Thus, we decided to hang another scroll in place of the stained-glass window, a black watercolor of mountains and water representing new opportunities and tranquillity. The new scroll was on the future side of the room, the perfect place for new vistas.

An arrangement of stones in a bowl topped by an Etruscan bronze is actually a gentle-running fountain. Earth, metal, fire, wind, and water are all present in this altar.

I also suggested hanging a pair of crystals in the front bay window to catch the afternoon sun. Rainbow hues reflected from crystals are great healers of space. Eliza was amazed that a small crystal from her bedroom window could project light all the way down her hallway and onto the front door. Before the days of electric lights, mirrors and crystals in particular were held in greater esteem than they are today, and it is easy to see why. Reflecting the rays of the sun in an unlit room or in a room illuminated only by lamplight, they can have a spectacular effect.

Returning to the living room, Eliza showed me her "husband altar" in the wealth and power corner. She did not use that term or even think of it in that way until I suggested it, nor did I recognize it as such until she told me about the objects. On a beautiful chest was placed a lamp and a small fountain filled with smooth black stones. On top of the stones rested a small Etruscan sculpture. All the objects, including the two paintings that hung above, had belonged to her late husband. Only a candle with two tassels had been added to the grouping. It was a fitting and dignified memorial, and yet it had none of the somberness usually associated with such a place. The sculpture was of a nude acrobat bent over backward as if to perform some feat of balance or trick for his ancient patrons.

"Julian always took care of me," Eliza said quietly. "He's still taking care of me." ■

A lamppost that bears a plaque in memory of Eliza's husband stands at the edge of Gramercy Park, across from her building.

16

U R B A N   S A L V A G E

So common has it become to find beautiful or rare objects in New York City's trash that such pieces now have their own genre, known as salvaged art. Furniture designer James Hong's collection of contemporary chairs is an excellent case in point. His apartment is populated with chairs by Corbusier, Mies van der Rohe, Saarinen, Warren MacArthur, and Joe Colombo, all plucked from curbside piles.

"I find other things as well, not only chairs," explained James. "But chairs sort of come to me. And, of course, a lot of these I have to restore, depending on what state I find them in. I know what I'm capable of, so I'll see a piece that's in the garbage, and I'll know I can bring it home and fix it up."

James's loft occupies the top floor of a small building on the Lower East Side. Going up a single flight of stairs, I found myself in the center of his apartment—and in the warm glow of sunlight streaming in from an old-fashioned skylight directly above. Although I had noticed that it was a two-story building, the skylight still came as a pleasant surprise. The ba-gua designates the center of a space as the health position, making it an excellent spot for a skylight. James had added a touch of whimsy, mounting a basketball hoop just inside the

OPPOSITE **Unconventional curtains of stretched nylon filter the ch'i and block a poor view while admitting light and air. The purple piano was suggested by a magazine ad for Bombay gin. Purple is the color of fortune.**

skylight rim. That, too, was appropriate for the health position; he actually worked out shooting hoops.

According to feng shui, the wall opposite the front door—the first thing you see upon entering a space—is always the fame wall. This is an important area, particularly for professionals who work at home. James sees clients in his apartment, and so we created a conference area to show off his designs as well as to create a welcoming area where he could converse. The centerpiece is a glass-top table with a white lacquer base that he designed. The collection of chairs around it includes one of his own; the others are salvaged pieces by Jacobsen, Saarinen, and Colombo. Because the space overall was already so eclectic the diverse chairs did not have the appearance of being mismatched.

The fame wall is the first area one sees upon entering a space, an important area for professionals who work out of their home. Here we have a conference setting composed of chairs of different designers grouped around one of James's tables.

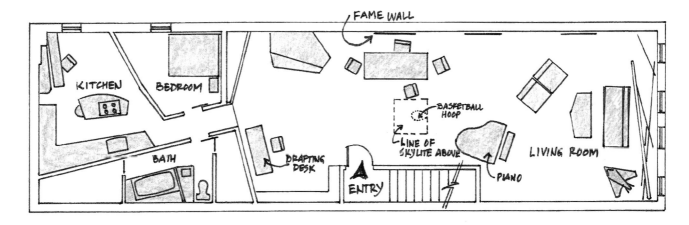

The most spectacular part of James's space is the northern end, which terminates in tall, old fashioned windows that each open on central pivots. James explained: "The pivots created a problem. Venetian blinds or some kind of material right up against the window would prevent them from opening. I had to consider something far enough away from the windows so that they could be opened and cleaned."

His solution was long stretches of white nylon hung from a large semicircular frame set in from the windows. Mounted on the children and future wall, these unusual curtains emphasize light and flow gently with the breeze. The physical attribute associated with this area is the lake, and I could not help but see these long stretches of white fabric as billowing sails.

In front of the swaths of white nylon is another sitting area around a slate coffee table, also of James's design. The top has five sides, so the angles of some of the corners are greater than ninety

Floor plan of James's space after changes.

ABOVE **The healing power of a rainbow is evoked in the coloration of James's floor. It also disguises the poor-quality pine typical of lofts originally designed for manufacturing. The steel frame of Mies van der Rohe's Barcelona chair is used as sculpture.**

ABOVE RIGHT **Three "salvaged" chairs, orphans from the street, are grouped in the children/creativity area. Left to right, a Mies van der Rohe, a Warren MacArthur, and a Giuseppe Terragni. The pointed aluminum and granite pieces in the marriage/relationship corner connote fire or passion.**

degrees and thus less angular. The ba-gua, of course, is an excellent example of "soft" corners, having angles of only forty-five degrees. That is not to say that sharp corners are necessarily negative. James has a pair of contemporary sculpture pieces that are basically five-foot spikes of steel and granite. After placing the pair in several different locations, we decided that they looked best in the marriage/relationship corner. Normally, sharp corners are avoided in this area, but they worked here for two reasons. First, the spikes pointed up, not toward any area of the room. Second, the overall form of both pieces was triangular. Triangles in feng shui connote fire. Thus these two spikes may be seen as adding passion to the marriage/relationship corner.

Moving toward the back of the loft, we come to James's work area in the knowledge corner of the main space. The protective walls of books give the little "cubbyhole" an enclosed, yin feeling. On the bottom shelves we see more evidence of whimsy in his collection of old cameras and typewriters. The interesting aspect of this area is the drafting table, which is facing the wall. As we have seen, desks and worktables should be turned to face the room. However, for some designers drafting tables are more like canvas walls than tabletops or traditional working surfaces. They are, for instance, often used with their surfaces vertical rather than horizontal. A vertical drafting surface placed facing the rest of the room would have the effect of cutting one off from the remainder of the space rather than giving perspective to it.

Placement of the drafting table against the wall also takes up less space and makes it less intrusive. "The drafting table is what I use to get my work done. I don't necessarily want to emphasize that to my clients. I want it to seem, at least from the outside, to be less

Space considerations forced a drafting table against the wall instead of facing toward the rest of the room. Corrective measures, which James should take, include placing a mirror or reflective strip on the wall directly above the table or hanging a wind chime at the door to symbolically warn of entry.

significant. I don't want to tell you, 'Oh Ron, I've been up all night working for you.' I want to say, 'Here's the design, here's the object.' And you say, 'Oh, it's wonderful.' And I say, 'Oh, it's no problem. It's no sweat.'"

Toward the rear of the loft we come to the bathroom. The shower is paneled in different shades of gray cement with a textured glass panel. The sink has a burgundy-colored marble top with a copper basin of a most unusual design. The basin's flat bottom simply slants from the right down to the left. No drain is apparent. The water seemingly runs into a crack at the deepest part. "The water mysteriously disappears," explains James. "Without a drain hole you don't immediately perceive exactly where that happens. One of the things I try to do in my work is to imbue things with more interest than the everyday about them—to make something a little more magical and special. To me that enhances the quality and the spirit of what people do in their everyday lives."

The trapezoidal shape of the countertop contains sharp angles, some more acute than ninety degrees. James countered these angles with the sink basin, also a trapezoid, by mounting the basin so that it seems to cut off the problematic corners. Also, the textured glass panel that partitions off the tub helps to soften the area. Still, I advised James that plants or other softening influences should be used to minimize the cutting impression of the sink.

One thing to be avoided in the presence of sharp angles is any feeling of cramped or constricted space. While the bathroom wasn't

The sharp angle of this sink is mitigated somewhat by the line of the inset copper basin. Any angle less than ninety degrees is considered a knife point and generates negative energy. Plants and the softness of the textured glass also help.

small, the presence of a conventional door, swinging inward, would have exaggerated the symbolic peril of the sharp edge of the sink. James's solution was to install aluminum pocket doors, sliding partitions that are quite thin and seem to disappear when in the open position.

At the far end of the loft we come to the kitchen, appropriately in the wealth and power corner. Although James doesn't cook a great deal, much of his income derives from designing kitchens. An over-

A breakfast nook for two has been
built into the relationship corner
using salvaged stainless-steel fixtures.
James sits on the green bench, which
allows a view of the room. The metal
chair in front is for guests.

OPPOSITE Greens and golds mark the
kitchen in the wealth and power corner. Colors of prosperity, as opposed
to fire, are significant since James frequently designs kitchens. The burners
and wok are on an island, allowing
for a view of the room while cooking.

hang shelters the sinks on the left; the stove (the fire center) is on an
island in the middle of the room. Both the cool green of the overhang and the brushed gold of the fixtures symbolize prosperity. The
kitchen island is freestanding with a movable wok. Black slate coun-
tertops give the island a feeling of stability.

A cozy breakfast niche resides in the relationship corner of the
kitchen (which is also the relationship corner for the entire building).
Here we see more of James's salvaged art. Stainless-steel fixtures
from an old diner have been transformed into a table and chair set
that seems both modern and nostalgic at the same time. In keeping
with the diner quality, a classic waffle iron has a permanent place on
the counter. The swivel seat in front is for guests. James prefers to sit
against the wall where he can see his creations. All the objects were
chosen for their history as well as their design, and their future is now
irrevocably altered. According to feng shui, the history of an object
remains with it always. ■

17

YIN AND YANG:
THE DIALOGUE

SoHo, located in lower Manhattan south of Houston Street, is a mecca for designers and artists. One can feel there a passion for art and originality. At eye level, galleries and shops are full of designer items and historical pieces. Above the shops—well, it seems that everyone in SoHo is upstairs, creating in their lofts, including the architect Michael McDonough and Corinne Trang, the producing editor of *Saveur* magazine.

Passing through Michael and Corinne's long entrance hallway, we seem suddenly to be in the center of their spacious loft. A large kitchen is to the left and a huge work space is to the right, with drafting tables, models, and computers. Dividing the loft overhead is a large structural beam, and beneath that beam rests a substantial round table with chairs. It is immediately clear that this configuration, in the middle of the apartment (the "self" area as designated by the ba-gua), is both a place of great importance and great problems.

The reason Michael and Corinne wanted a consultation was to help them decide on a place to carve out another room in the loft. They wanted to try a feng shui approach. "We like the depth and maturity of the Asian cultures," Michael told me. As I looked at the area I saw that it was indeed large but it was also full. Someone would

OPPOSITE **A wind instrument of bamboo helps disperse the negative energy of the divisive beam. The tubular screen evokes a fluted column to support the beam. The round shape of the table symbolizes that all who sit there do so as equals.**

have to give up something if space were to be found for another room.

We sat at the round table (designed by Michael) to discuss the new room, and I commented first on the overhead beam. It divided the office area, a yang, active, and expansive space, from the more enclosed, yin space of the kitchen. The separation was not a problem—in fact, it was a good idea—but why place the table beneath the beam? We explored moving the table but it was not a small piece, and it seemed there was no other place for it to go. We finally agreed that because of floor plan limitations, it had to be placed beneath the beam. We then considered what cures were available to keep the beam from being divisive or having a negative effect on communication that took place at the table below. I felt this was terribly important because, as in most households, those issues that *really* have to be discussed are talked about around the kitchen table, not, for example, in the living room.

Corinne had found a contemporary screen made of varying lengths of aluminum tubing that could be used to divide the office area from the table. This was certainly the correct approach, as the table was more closely associated with the kitchen area than the office. Designed by Glendon Good, the screen, titled *Poseidon,* was quite flexible and could be molded to any contour. Better still, the gentle curvature of its upper edge was definitely yin. Of equal importance was the impression of strength the screen seemed to impart. The verticality of the tubes gave the illusion of a great fluted column.

It was as if a phantom pillar encompassed the table and by virtue of its own strength held back the overhead beam.

To offset the effect of an overhead beam, the traditional feng shui solution is to mount two bamboo flutes on or under the beam at angles to suggest the upper half of the ba-gua. Also, the flutes should be hung so that the mouthpieces are on the bottom. It is thought that the breath from the instrument pushes back the energy of the beams. Two red tassels are also hung on each flute to evoke firecrackers, which are thought to break up negative energy with their explosions. Our solution was to hang only a single Chinese wind instrument, a kind of exotic panpipes made of bamboo (found

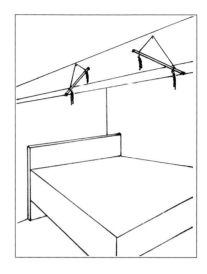

ABOVE **Traditionally, two flutes mounted at the proper angles and the proper distance from the walls symbolically uplift offending beams by suggesting the top part of the ba-gua.**

LEFT **Floor plan of Michael and Corinne's loft apartment.**

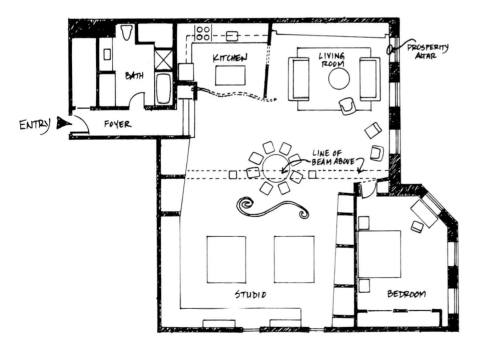

in an Asian art gallery), directly above the table. Its large size in combination with the suggestion of a column from the tubular screen seemed sufficient to control the energy of the beam. We did, however, strengthen the instrument with the traditional red tassels. It was also agreed that for optimal conditions plants or cuttings should always appear on the table in a tall, round Chinese water jug. The round (yin) shape of the jug strengthened the association with the kitchen area and echoed our phantom column that supported the beam.

A great deal of the consultation was spent discussing the table/beam area because it was central both to the space and to Michael and Corinne's life together. It marked the place where the two of them met as equals, for there is no head at a round table, so all who sit at it are symbolically equal.

Next we considered the kitchen, a beautiful space designed by Michael, on the family side of the loft. Definitely a yin area, it was demarcated partly by a gentle curved overhang. Because it was neither straight nor structural, this configuration did not have the negative energy of a beam. The stove against the wall, however, was a problem, and Corinne decided on a traditional cure to give herself a view of the rest of the kitchen. A wok with a highly polished lid was placed permanently on the stove. A stainless-steel teapot was also pressed into service for this purpose.

Overall, the kitchen seemed to me one of the best places in the loft, where the creative energies of these two people came together,

ABOVE **The color of food. Corinne is a food editor and writes cookbooks. Here are the ingredients of a Vietnamese dish consisting of orange dried shrimp, green scallions, ocher lily buds, black wood ears, yellow ginger, and red chile. Colorful food is symbolic of a greater enjoyment of life.**

LEFT **The curved overhang emphasizes the yin quality of the kitchen, which was designed by Michael. The incorrect placement of the stove should be accommodated by reflective surfaces.**

since Michael had designed the space and Corinne used it domestically and professionally. Corinne, a food editor who was writing a cookbook, was preparing a number of Vietnamese family recipes.

The living room area is beyond the kitchen and in the wealth and power corner. Such a placement often indicates that those who occupy the space consider their greatest wealth to be their friends. The gentle yin shape of the couch (designed by Robert Venturi), the

table, and the chairs clearly welcome friends, and the care with which the items were selected and placed is an indication of the esteem in which they are held. The textures of the materials are soft, luxuriant, and nurturing. The green leather lounge chair, the "McEasy," was designed by Michael. It was, to my surprise, a rocking chair.

Both Corinne and Michael had indicated a need to promote their design business. After reviewing the rest of the space, I recommended adding an altar in the wealth and power corner. As we discussed various options, I learned that plants did not do particularly well in that part of the loft, and they felt a water fountain would be too large. We agreed, therefore, on a traditional window altar composed of a rice bowl in combination with bamboo flutes, echoing the bamboo and musical instruments in other parts of the space.

The bowl we chose was one of Corinne and Michael's favorite objects, a hand-carved piece from Africa. Filling it with uncooked white rice for prosperity, we inserted into it nine red envelopes, each containing a sample of foreign currency, to symbolize their revenues from exports, an area they hoped to expand. Water was held in an octagonal gold-rimmed glass by William Goldsmith, a glass artist.

The bamboo flutes were employed in their traditional role as symbols of strengthening or future prosperity. The four Western elements of the altar were represented by the red envelopes (fire), bamboo (air), rice (earth), and water cup (water).

In the marriage/relationship corner I was struck by a grouping that I recognized at once as a metaphor for the relationship of these

OPPOSITE **This welcoming seating arrangement in the wealth and power corner indicates the couple's wealth in their friends.**

To enhance prospects for a new export business, a small altar in the wealth and power corner was constructed containing an African bowl filled with uncooked rice and nine red envelopes, each containing a sample of foreign currency.

two creative people: a pair of chairs together as if in conversation. One had bright contrasts and color; the other was understated with simple, elegant lines. The more colorful one was a Kim MacConnell (1977); the other was an American Craftsman style of the early twentieth century. I strongly urged them to leave these two chairs together for their symbolic value. Above them, a polished aluminum round mirror, connoting compassion, wholeness, and completeness, was rehung at eye level.

The bedroom entrance is in the marriage/relationship corner of the living room. His and her chairs create a welcoming niche at this important juncture. Brass Soleri bells, hanging beside the door, help correct the improper bed placement.

This quiet yin bedroom contrasts with the "busyness" of the studio work space outside.

The bedroom, which we entered next, was mostly of Michael's design, including a solid wall of cabinetry and storage space. However, it was a tiny children's chair below the window that struck me first. Designed by Michael, it was made entirely of recycled newspapers and reflected both his and Corinne's concerns for ecology. Between the two windows a large painting, a twentieth-century contemporary, was Michael's, and it was flanked by an African fertility goddess and a Thai water jar that were Corinne's. Also close by were a pair of Indonesian coconut masks in which the female mask happened to be bigger than the male mask. I recommended placing a stalk of large bamboo in the corner to echo the altar in the wealth and power corner, thereby symbolically balancing their prosperity and their relationship. Some smaller interesting pieces of erotic art belonged to both Michael and Corinne.

The only thing in the bedroom that needed to be changed was

A Gustave Stickley library table, serving as a desk, was shifted to the knowledge side of the bedroom so as not to restrict the career area. It was thoughtfully balanced by Michael and Corinne: her standing lamp for his Noguchi lamp, her Japanese print for his Outsider art.

OPPOSITE Yin and yang are balanced by the round table in the center of the space with the "uplifting" bamboo flute.

the small desk. Actually a Gustave Stickley library table, it was located on the career wall, too close to both the door and the bed. Any kind of cramping or restriction in the career area is not a good idea because it is thought to restrict the work flow. Shifting it to the nearest window placed it in the knowledge corner. The items on the surface were mostly Michael's, including a small Noguchi lamp and an orange print of two horses, an example of Outsider art. Corrine's objects included a Brera lamp (the oval lamp on a pole), which had definite feminine connotations, and a Japanese print.

Returning to the main work area, which was on the children/creativity side of the loft, the perfect location for a creative work space, I was treated to a number of chair designs still in process. Large square shelves contained objects collected by Michael and Corinne, including some American Indian pottery, from which they often drew inspiration in their work. The area was energized by light from tall windows and the presence of several computers.

When I spoke to Michael about his reasons for using feng shui, he said, "I feel that the core of feng shui is really making people much more aware of how they *care* for their space, which ultimately shows how all of us care for ourselves. In architecture and design we sometimes forget those reasons. Feng shui helps us to remember."

At the end of the photo session, we decided to clear the work area and roll up the screen in order to take a shot that gave an overall perspective of as much of the loft as possible. In the photograph you can see the large red scroll at the entrance of their apartment. It

The work area is appropriately on the children/creativity side of the loft. Chairs, one of Michael's interests, are studied in model form. This is also known as the future area.

is a rubbing from a stone tablet in Xian, a traditional pattern known as 100 Ways of Saying Happiness. The scroll made me think about the difficulty of two people, both designers, finding and keeping happiness in such a highly competitive profession.

In feng shui happiness is achieved through balance. If one

member of the couple dominates the work space, then perhaps the other dominates the kitchen and the family corner, or if he dominates the bedroom in the marriage corner, then she dominates the living room in the wealth and power corner.

Maintaining balance in a relationship, especially in the twenty-first century, means communication. When two highly gifted, articulate people come together, the equalness of their relationship makes communication imperative. This dialogue of yin and yang can be expressed, even encouraged, in the layout and arrangement of a space.

When I first met with Michael and Corinne, they were not married, but had been living together comfortably for some time. A month after the consultation I returned for a visit to find that they had become man and wife. Corinne had also secured a new job, and Michael had gained several new projects from major clients. Both spoke of the discussions they had had following my first visit. These discussions, about their aspirations and how these aspirations might be reflected in their space, had precipitated the changes. We became so interested in this aspect of the consultation that we never got around to deciding where to put the extra room they'd originally called me about. Next time . . . ■

PART THREE

FENG SHUI CURES

18

P R A C T I C A L
A P P L I C A T I O N S

Finding effective cures and applying them properly is central to the practice of feng shui. What do you do to improve your chances of getting a job, selling a house, or finding romance? Sometimes the remedies are simple and uncomplicated and involve only moving a piece of furniture or repositioning a picture on a wall. At other times, and when the budget permits, new construction, landscaping, or even demolition is necessary. Most of the time, however, people want to make as few alterations to their space as possible, so a cure must be introduced. A cure involves bringing in an object that will alter the energy of a space and create new and beneficial associations in the mind of the occupant.

Mirrors are a good example of a feng shui cure. They reflect energy; they offer new vistas; they welcome; and they augment whatever they reflect. Mirrors can effect a whole host of corrections. In fact, they are so frequently prescribed as cures that they have been called "the aspirin of feng shui." In psychology mirrors are a metaphor for introspection; in myths and fairy tales they usually symbolize a deeper understanding of the self; and in feng shui the space one occupies is thought of as a mirror of the self.

There are two distinct aspects to a cure: the tangible (or objec-

OPPOSITE **Objects from nature are natural feng shui cures.**

tive) and the intangible (or subjective). Let's say that a man's business is failing. He works out of his home. Perhaps I will find that his desk is in a poor spot to support his business endeavors. The view may be onto a vacant lot that has negative connotations for him. Perhaps he intended to build on that lot but never raised the capital. Every time he looks out and sees the lot he thinks, "Another one of my failures" and a sense of inadequacy is reinforced.

Relocating the desk gives him a different view. The omnipresent symbol of failure is gone and, more important, the new view reminds him of his resolve to do better. Now every time he enters his home office and sees the desk in its new position, he knows why it is there, and it prods him to act on his resolve. Maybe I ought to get those invoices out before the holidays, he thinks. And he sits down and does a task he might have put off without the gentle reminder of his desk. This is the tangible or logical aspect of a cure.

The other, intangible part of the cure is the man's *belief* that this change will have an effect. It may give him added confidence. He may use a more positive tone when he speaks to his clients or he may pursue new business opportunities with fresh assertiveness.

Any cure can have both tangible and intangible components in equal or unequal measure. The interesting thing is that the cures with the least amount of logic are often very effective. Thus, the intangible is not frosting on the cake but a powerful component of the cure. Perhaps that is because an intangible cure requires faith. It is easy, for example, to do something that makes sense to remedy a situation.

How many times have we taken a logical step knowing in our heart that it would do no good, and sure enough we were right. On the other hand, taking an intangible or subjective action requires a leap of faith, an assertion of will. That belief, that assertiveness, is very important to the success of a cure.

A word of caution is due here. Faith that a feng shui cure will work should stimulate *action*. Simply hanging a symbol for money in the wealth and power corner will not make you rich and famous without further effort on your part. Some people, for whom the faith part of the cure is easy, develop this passive, easy-way-out attitude, one guaranteed to produce a result: disappointment. If your belief stimulates you to action, then you have psyched yourself into a winning posture and your chances for success are greatly enhanced. If you have any doubts about this, talk to any football coach.

Through millennia of experience, feng shui practitioners have developed tools to aid in the practice of their craft. Our toolbox is full of cures, old and new, to bring about changes of one sort or another. Many of my tools are traditional or have definite associations with Chinese philosophies. But, though the Chinese seem preoccupied with symbols, they by no means have the market cornered. Symbols from other cultures are just as valid, often more so depending on the client's background. For example, Western symbols such as a cornucopia for plenty or a laurel wreath for victory may be used as cures just as easily as a ba-gua mirror for protection or bamboo flutes for strength, or peace.

MIRRORS

Mirrors provide the eye with opportunities for a change of focus, easing eye muscles, which, in turn, relieves tension and promotes relaxation. High-quality images of ourselves, such as those provided by mirrors, contribute to our self-respect and our personal sense of well-being. Mirrors open new vistas psychologically and create new opportunities. Long used as security devices, mirrors have increased our personal safety. Although inexpensive and commonplace, mirrors make a substantial contribution to the quality of our lives. If, for some reason, a mirror is not practical, then an object of polished metal, or even a piece of foil, can sometimes be used.

The shape of a mirror, including its frame, relates directly to its meaning and to its usefulness as a cure. Round mirrors connote love, completeness, and wholeness. They are particularly appropriate for the marriage/relationship corner or those areas representing children, family, or helpful people. A round mirror within a square frame symbolizes the balance of heaven and earth, particularly appropriate for the marriage/relationship corner and also for the family wall. A square mirror within a round frame resembles a traditional Chinese coin, a symbol of prosperity. This is a strong symbol appropriate to the wealth and power corner or the family wall. An eight-sided mirror, representative of the ba-gua, can be used to add good fortune to any area in which it is placed.

Mirrors have been traditionally used to compensate for problematic placements in the home, particularly of major pieces like

beds, desks, and stoves. Placed on the future wall a mirror offers a view symbolizing a peaceful and serene future. If your bed is squeezed into a small room, a mirror at the headboard will open your sleeping quarters to more opportunities. However, mirrors placed along the side of the bed are thought to disrupt sleep. In cramped spaces a mirror reduces stress by making a room feel more spacious and accommodating while at the same time offering additional views of the furnishings. When mirrors are inappropriate or unavailable, any reflective surface will do. In the West, stoves are often placed facing a wall so that reflective surfaces are necessary to give the person cooking visual access to the rest of the room. In traditional feng shui reflective objects, whether mirrors or teapots, are thought to keep the cook from being caught off guard. As food preparation is central to the well-being of the family, an adequate view for the cook means an adequate perspective on the future of the family.

LIGHT

Cures that actually generate light, as opposed to reflecting it, such as a desk lamp or linear strips of light mounted under the kitchen cabinets over the countertop, can enhance your focus for a task at hand, whatever that task may be, and contribute to its successful completion. Whenever you lighten dark corners or brighten your room in general, you are symbolically bringing sunlight into the area. All kinds of artificial light enrich our interiors: task-specific lighting provided by a desk lamp, general lighting from a standing floor or ceil-

ing light, or decorative bulbs. The bowl of white electrified Christmas lights seen here is typical of a "transcendental" cure. To enhance prosperity, one could place this bowl in the wealth and power corner. The lights should be plugged into a timer so that they energize the corner twice a day for two hours, from 11:00 to 1:00. Noon and midnight are considered particularly auspicious times of day.

COLORS

Colors have associations and emotional impact that relate to specific objects and shapes; often these associations are culture-dependent. For example, red represents good luck to the Chinese, and it connotes the passion of Christ to Christians. In China the color yellow is associated with the emperor; in the West yellow strands surround a car accident or tragedy, or it symbolizes quarantine. White represents purity and virginity in traditional Western wedding gowns; in the Orient, white is the color of mourning.

Red: The color of luck. As such it is used for celebrations such as birthdays and New Year's. In China the word *luck* carries a slightly different meaning than it does in the West, being more akin to what we think of as good fortune. On the ba-gua red is the color associated with the fame wall, and it carries connotations of strength, energy, and sexual power. Gods used as guardians for doorways are often shown with red skin to incorporate the power of fire. Red is yang and signifies success and virtue. Red pomegranates symbolize fertility, love, and hope.

Yellow: The color of the emperors during the Ch'ing dynasty (1644–1912). Pu Yi, the last emperor, said in his memoirs that in his childhood he remembered seeing yellow everywhere. On the ba-gua it is the color of the center position standing, for self and health. It is, of course, the color of gold, so it is associated with wealth. In the West gold also connotes power and is often used for emblems of office.

Green: The color of exuberant growth, future prosperity, health, and tranquillity. On the ba-gua it represents the family and is considered a lucky color for children.

Brown: Associated with stability and depth. Once the color of emperors (Sung dynasty, 960–1279), it is often chosen as a color of contemplation. As a color of meditation it is appropriate for the knowledge and spirituality corner.

Pink: Connotes love, joy, happiness, and romance. On the ba-gua it is associated with the marriage/relationship corner.

Blue: Because of its associations with sky and water, blue symbolizes spirituality and depth of understanding. It is the color of tranquillity and composure. Sometimes it is the color of mystery, and in its darkest shades it is a symbol of death. On the ba-gua it is the color of the career and travel corner, and in its stronger, purple shades it is identified with the wealth and power corner.

SOUND

Sound is an important cure because it can convey its message even when we are asleep. It is the medium of alarm, and yet it is also one

of the most comforting of the senses. Sounds from nature, such as the rustle of leaves or the tinkling of a wind chime, promote relaxation and composure.

All water sounds are thought to be soothing, whether surf, rain, or the gentle splashing of a fountain. Recently, indoor fountains have become popular both in conjunction with feng shui and simply as home decorations. The motion of the water in a fountain or pond creates a benevolent stirring of the ch'i.

SCENT

It has long been known that the sense of smell has the power to evoke personal recollections and memories. Specific moods, too, are within the purview of fragrance: for example, perfume is thought to stir the passions. In the East, incense is believed to keep homes and sacred places free of evil spirits; it is linked with purity and the ascent of the spirit into the heavens. Lavender is thought to soothe the temperament and sweet grass to clear the mind. The best location for incense or other sources of fragrance is the center of the room, the earth position.

TOUCH

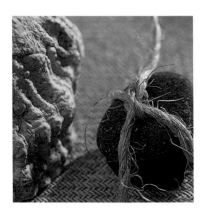

We speak of the feel of something as a way of describing how we think about it. Sight, too, plays a role in the sense of touch, as the visual impression of a texture may give us the same or similar impression as physical contact. The actual feel of an object is important when it is close at hand and likely to be touched, such as doors, furniture, or items on a personal altar. We also touch with our feet, so the texture of floors and floor coverings is important, particularly in the bedroom and bathroom.

CURES FROM NATURE

Natural objects ground us with our own experiences in the real world. A bird's nest, a flower, a piece of fruit, a natural crystal, a shell, all have come into being independent of the efforts or the desires of man. Each has a quality and a richness that man-made objects cannot duplicate.

Bird's nests: We are humbled by the discovery of the ultimate yin structure, a nest. Who among us could build such a thing, or who has conceived a design so elegant as an egg?

Flowers: For millennia people have given flowers to convey, one human being to another, thoughts of love, remembrance, health, peace, or forgiveness. Even in the graves of Neanderthal men the remains of flowers have been found. Cultivated in front of a home, flowers signify prosperity and a regard for others and for one's self. In this city scene a bare window with a view of other buildings is transformed by their presence.

Table centerpieces: Whether for the gods or guests, offerings convey wishes. Fruit signifies a wish for prosperity and bamboo for the continuation of that prosperity into the future. Bamboo also provides strength that can hold prosperity. Placement in the center of

the room means that the wish is for abundant health and happiness; in the wealth and power corner it would encourage the accumulation of tangible wealth.

Wealth comes in many sizes and shapes. The square bowl within the frame of the round coffee table echoes the form of the traditional Chinese coin, which is always a symbol of money and prosperity.

Earth Crystals: Great energy is thought to reside in crystals, yet as a product of the earth they signify stability. Any area that needs energizing will benefit from the addition of crystals, particularly if located in places where they can refract natural light. Compared to a man-made crystal, natural crystals are more subtle, complex, and, in the long run, stronger.

JUGGLING THE ELEMENTS

In traditional Chinese thinking the world is made up of five elements: earth, metal, water, wood, and fire. This classification has nothing to do with scientific categories based on atomic structure, it is simply a way of viewing the world, a symbolic framework that can be helpful when proposing cures for a room, house, or a site. "Balancing the elements" does not refer to the proportion in which these elements are present at a site; it refers only to the use of some of these elements to modify or contrast with others.

Fire: The most yang of all elements, fire brings with it maximum energy, and so it should be introduced with thoughtfulness and care. In traditional feng shui it is the element associated with success; thus a candle in an area in which you seek to succeed is a strong and excellent cure. Fire is the element of summer; its energy rises, and it is associated with the direction south. In the ideal feng shui site the view is to the south, the red phoenix view. In almost every culture fire is a symbol of worship, transformation, or remembrance. No altar should be without the element of fire.

Wood: Spring is the time of wood. It represents growth and expansion in all directions. Whereas the energy of fire rises and is spent quickly, the energy of wood is longer-lasting, like the growth of a tree, which is upward, outward, and downward all at the same time. Birth and new beginnings are the connotations of wood. Often its use as a symbol is more appropriate than fire because it endures longer.

Earth: The central element and the nourisher of all things, earth has no season of its own but provides for the transition from one season to the next. As the ultimate provider, it is the symbol of accumulation. Appropriate to its central position, its color is yellow. As a cure, earth is used to symbolize change; thus, in the career position it would symbolize the desire for a new position or a change of jobs.

Metal: Harvest is the time of metal. It is the symbol of completeness and fulfillment. The altar of a mature person might appropriately be dominated by this element; for others it might express a desire for stability. As the densest of elements metal is the symbol of coming together and introspection. It is represented by the color

white, although in the West its colors might appropriately be yellow, orange, or red. Its direction is that of the setting sun.

Water: Winter is the time of water and its direction is north. Water is the symbol of maximum introspection and of the resolution of all things. Blue and black are its colors, and it is also the symbol of purification, patience, and ultimate peace. It is the most yin of all elements and in many ways the most complex. In its depths it has the capacity to absorb negative energy, and it is this cleansing role that it is most often employed in a cure. At its most positive, water is a sign of abundance and a vehicle for life or the *promise* of life.

TRADITIONAL FENG SHUI CURES

To westerners some of the traditional feng shui cures, such as ba-guas and talismans, have the appearance of five-and-dime trinkets. But if one travels to the Far East one sees these traditional symbols in the homes of both the rich and the poor, and in businesses large and small. Where the symbols are recognized their significance far outweighs their cost and even the care with which they are made. What I stress to my clients is that the associations one has with the cure, icon, or symbol are important, not its cost. Whatever cure you use, whether it be the subtle introduction of an element onto a table arrangement or a brightly painted ba-gua, it need only be the right one for you.

The medallion: As enlightened as he is fierce, this monster has a ba-gua as his third eye. The crossed swords signify protection, and so this little fellow might be pressed into service guarding a doorway or facing the direction of possible danger or disturbance.

Chinese mirrors: Reflective surfaces do more than mirror reality; they may also alter it. This feature has been used in traditional feng shui to counter difficult problems about which little can be done. For example, concave mirrors make things appear smaller and upside down. The influence of a nearby house or building that dominates its neighbors can be reduced by the placement of a concave mirror. You may smile as you leave your home knowing that in a way you have cut an aggressive neighbor down to size and turned him on his head. Convex mirrors enlarge the size of the area reflected and are excellent security devices.

Both the ba-guas and the door guardians shown here have mirrors that reflect negative influences and energies back to their sources. The value is only symbolic, of course, but they can serve as reminders to be careful as you enter or leave your home or they can cheerfully reassure you that all is well, which might, in turn, reduce the stress that builds in the course of an ordinary day.

Red envelopes: Any happy or auspicious occasion, such as birthdays, weddings, and New Year's is a time to use red envelopes. Payment to a feng shui consultant is always in a red envelope to signify that the interchange is of the highest order. In one direction flows wisdom and advice, in the other, a most powerful medium of exchange.

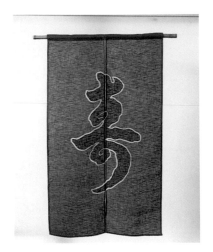

Wind chimes: Because they produce sound, wind chimes can serve as warning devices as well as markers of welcome. Indoors they are used as a cure when the placement of a bed or desk keeps the occupant from seeing the entry to the room. The thoughtful guest will announce his presence by touching the chime, or an intruder may inadvertently brush against it, alerting the occupant to his presence.

In the photograph on the top left we have a Tibetan bell-chime and an inexpensive set made of Chinese brass.

Chinese coins: Traditional Chinese coins have always been symbols of good fortune. Individually they are used as charms. Hung in strings of ten they represent the ten traditional dynasties, or "ten emperors" as they are called, thought to bring luck and good fortune. In any form they are thought to enhance prosperity.

Norens: These lengths of cloth are used when the energy from

a hallway or the activity in an adjacent area threatens to intrude into a room. A noren is a simple and beautiful way of screening such an entryway without closing it completely.

Bamboo Flutes: In Chinese classical music the flute is always the instrument that conveys good news. Crossed flutes are less aggressive symbols of protection than crossed swords. In Chinese businesses you may see them over the cash register. The bamboo from which they are made is a symbol of future prosperity and good ch'i.

Handmade Crystals: From earliest times cut crystals were highly prized and thought to possess magical properties. I use crystals often in my own teaching to transform energy, usually sunlight, into a healing rainbow of colors.

Crystals are also excellent objects of focus for meditation. Visualizations that make use of crystals are for the transformation of negative energies into positive ones.

PROBLEMS AND SOLUTIONS

Here are a few examples of real-life problems to illustrate how the cures might be put to use. But please remember that feng shui cures are flexible and have different dynamics depending on circumstance. What is an effective cure one day may be ineffectual at another time. Spaces change, circumstances change, and—most important—people change.

Problem: *A family is considering buying a beautiful two-story home; the main stairway from the second floor descends to the ground floor in a direct line to the front door. In traditional feng shui this configuration causes the good fortune of a family to escape from the house too quickly.*

Solution: The energy coming down the stairs does not need to be stopped, only slowed, perhaps fragmented, and, most desirably, directed back into the rest of the house. I recommended hanging a chandelier between the door and the end of the stairs. Crystals fragment energy. Two plants placed on either side of the door inside could absorb some of the energy. Because the floor was highly polished wood, I recommended a thick carpet for the foyer to slow the movement of the ch'i toward the door. A mirror on one wall of the foyer redirects the energy to other parts of the house.

■

Problem: *An urban family town house adjoins a funeral home. The wife feels that the presence of the funeral home is affecting her outlook on life.*

Solution: Since the construction of the dividing wall was actually a shared load-bearing masonry wall (known as a party wall), the intention was to energetically separate the two properties, literally the yin house (funeral home) from the yang house (the family home). I proposed three cures. First, linear skylights were installed along the wall next to the funeral home to bring light into the area of most concern. Next, floor-to-ceiling mirrors were mounted to amplify the light, bring in the energy of the sky, and energetically open up the area (making it more yang). Finally, plants were placed along the mirror below the skylight to invite natural life energy into the house, separating it from the dead energy next door.

■

MIRROR CURES

Problem: *I visit a couple whose teenage son is not doing well in school. Although he is a pleasant, young man, he seems unconcerned about his lack of achievement or his options for the future.*

Solution: After observing the layout of the young man's bedroom, I notice that his entry door faces a series of blank walls: one wall immediately faces the door of his room and one wall at the end of the hallway leads to the garage. I recommend placing a collegiate poster on the wall facing his bedroom door and a large mirror above a console table with fresh flowers on the wall located at the end of the hallway. Every time he goes to his car he will be reminded of the impression he is making on others, giving him a chance to reflect and readjust his attitude to a more confident and positive. By reducing stress, mirrors open up opportunities.

■

Problem: *A small room in a city apartment is dark and uninviting. Its only window faces onto an airshaft.*

Solution: Reflective surfaces can maximize the effect of available light. I recommended repainting the room in a glossy, light-colored enamel. The floors were natural wood, so a coat of high-gloss polyurethane was used. As a result, almost any light from the airshaft, no matter how dismal, will create a cheerful glow. A few reflective crystals on the windowsill also help distract from the uninspiring view. To keep the reflective surfaces from seeming too harsh under artificial light, lamps and fixtures using lower wattage bulbs, symbolically creating the luminescence of candlelight, were added.

■

COLOR CURES

Problem: *A woman has recently divorced. Her family has been in a state of turmoil and she longs to repair her relationships with her grown children. I ask her what room most exemplifies family to her. The living room, she answers.*

Solution: Green is the color associated with family. It is also a healing color with respect to nature and plants. In the living room I suggest that only the family wall be painted apple green. This striking color suggests growth and renewal and will encourage her to seek new and dynamic ways to strengthen her relationship with her children.

■

Problem: *A client's bathroom is in the wealth and power corner. It is difficult not to associate this location with flushing one's money down the toilet. Plumbing and other considerations make moving the bathroom prohibitively expensive for the client.*

Solution: In the West red is the color of a stop sign. Painting the wall behind the toilet and several accessories red is enough to provide a visual reminder to watch his finances. In addition, he should consciously close the toilet lid after each use.

■

SOUND CURES

Problem: *A couple wants to sell their apartment, but the real estate agent tells them that prospective owners find it lifeless.*

Solution: The backs of the armchairs faced visitors when they first walked into the living room, so I advised simply repositioning the chairs so that they welcomed guests. I also suggested the addition of nine potted lush green plants surrounding a small water fountain in the living room and a wind chime on the front door. The gentle splash of falling water and the tinkle of a wind chime fill the space with welcoming sounds and soften any harshness. A fixture that requires care, like a fountain, combined with plants, also gives the impression of pride and pleasure in living in a space. Potential buyers are attracted to these qualities.

■

Problem: *A woman living alone has become nervous and finds it difficult to concentrate. When I inquire about her family I find that her children, grandchildren, and even neighbors are accustomed to entering without knocking. She does not want to appear unloving or unfriendly and yet the coming and going of people at will makes her uncomfortable.*

Solution: I recommended replacing her walkways with pebble or crushed stone surfaces. Steps on crushed stone make an amazing amount of noise, enough to be heard from an upstairs bedroom. Surfacing her driveway with crushed stone would also help. I also suggested replacing the leather thong on the front gate be with a metal latch that clanks when open and shut, as well as putting delicate wind chimes just inside the front and back doors. Finally, I urged her *never* to oil the squeaky screen door on the back porch. These subtle and natural sources of sound will inform her of the presence of people on her property and yet not be perceived as alarms by her family or neighbors. These cures will add immeasurably to her sense of security.

■

SCENT CURES

Problem: *A woman was cited for poor job performance. In our consultation it became clear that she was suffering from a sense of low self-esteem.*

Solution: The doorway to her apartment was just beyond a garbage chute, and I remembered a faint smell of refuse just before reaching her door. I suggested that she line the door to the garbage chute with weather stripping so that random smells were less likely to escape into the hallway and affect her when entering or leaving the apartment. Next, I suggested she purchase scented candles or potpourri to give her apartment a special fragrance, as well as scented bath soaps. Gentle fragrances are an excellent way to encourage self-esteem and give one a feeling of self worth.

■

TOUCH CURES

Problem: *After they paint and redecorate, a couple finds their bedroom harsh and slightly uncomfortable.*

Solution: I suggest covering one wall of the bedroom with a tapestry from their travels to soften the hard surface of the painted walls. Throw rugs on each side of the bed will give them something soft to step out onto in the morning. Silk throw pillows for the bed and chairs were also suggested.

■

NATURE CURES

Problem: *A conflict in an office suite makes work uncomfortable for one of my clients. The supervisor, who is edgy and unfriendly, seems to set the tone for the office.*

Solution: I suggested that the employees chip in and buy fresh flowers for the common area of the suite for at least eighteen working days. Flowers are great humanizers, just the thing for uplifting the mood of the manager. Flowers also bring good luck!

■

Problem: *A couple in the suburbs is having difficulty with their neighbors. They have ceased to enjoy their house because of the hostility they can sense coming from their neighbors' house.*

Solution: I suggested reinforcing the fence between the two properties with shrubs of a kind that can grow reasonably tall. Plants are great absorbers of negative energy, but it is important that they be evergreens so that they can function as buffers in the winter as well. I also suggested growing colorful plants against the house on the same side, particularly under the windows in window boxes. This will reduce tensions and create a visual harmony between the neighbors.

■

Problem: *A therapist notices that the number of clients she sees has begun to decline. Though she has been enjoying her north-facing office for some time, the space is now beginning to feel downcast.*

Solution: Placing the ba-gua at the entry of her office, I found that the far left corner where she sat with her clients was dominated by an amethyst crystal (a good idea), which was, in turn, attended by several dying plants (not a good idea). A small light was placed directly behind the crystal to energize and highlight its brilliant quality. The plants were replaced by bamboo stalks. Dead plants symbolize neglect, but cut bamboo has an entirely different energy, symbolizing strength. Twenty-seven stalks in a wicker basket were arranged to radiate from the corner. Multiples of nine are powerful in feng shui. A large mirror was placed next to this arrangement to connote the expansion of opportunities for enhancing wealth. As a final touch we placed nine coins, each in a red envelope, into the basket. Now, every time she took her seat for a client session the confluence of these objects would suggest to her a positive outlook.

■

JUGGLING ELEMENTS

Problem: *A couple has just moved to a new home. The wife came from a neighborhood where she knew everyone and is depressed because she knows no one here. She is not sure how to establish relationships with the neighbors.*

Solution: I recommended the addition of a birdbath with a flagpole and colorful banner in the front yard. A birdbath ostensibly welcomes wildlife, a symbol of peace and tranquillity. Placing potted plants or planting a border of colorful flowers along the front walk signals to neighbors they are welcome. The combination of these elements—plants (earth), birdbath (water), flagpole (wood), colorful banner (fire)—is harmonizing and enhances ch'i.

■

Problem: *A middle-aged man was concerned about instability in his professional life. He had changed jobs many times and never seemed capable of focusing on any one profession.*

Solution: Based on the enhancing qualities of fire, earth, and metal, I suggested placing a vase of vibrant red flowers (fire and good luck) on a wrought-iron console table (metal) with a large earthen pot on the career wall near his entry door. Earth connotes stability and longevity. Its weight would anchor the area (career), and its position would remind him of his desire for stability as he came and went. He needed an umbrella stand anyway, and so the earthen jug was happily pressed into service.

■

TRADITIONAL CURES

Problem: *A couple whose house was at the end of a short, dead-end street was concerned about negative energy bombarding their home.*

Solution: I recommended placing a traditional ba-gua, with a mirror in the center, on the outside of their front door facing toward the street. The mirror reflects negative energy away from the house, and the octagon is an icon of protection.

■

Problem: *In a household where I consulted, financial matters were often neglected, threatening to destabilize the couple's relationship.*

Solution: I proposed hanging a string of ten emperor's coins in the wealth and power corner. On a field of bright, imperial yellow this Eastern icon of wealth and prosperity would remind all members of the family of their responsibility to care for their resources and to take seriously their financial obligations.

THE BLESSING
CEREMONY

Whenever there is a special emphasis or focus to a consultation, or a particularly important problem has come into focus, I sometimes recommend a feng shui blessing ceremony. A ceremony is especially helpful when moving into a new space to purge any negative history. Properties to be sold also benefit from a blessing ceremony, as these can be anxious times for the seller.

A blessing ceremony should be done after corrective measures have been taken in the arrangement of the furnishings or in the building of the home. Thus, during the ceremony, the specific cures adopted can be further vested with the associations designed to reinforce the aspirations of the owners, to correct problems, or to enhance the chances of success. A blessing ceremony can also be an event unto itself with no connections to a consultation.

The ceremony may be private or guests may be invited to witness or participate. The feng shui practitioner will usually take the participants into every accessible area of the residence (including the outdoors if a house) where the desired associations with the particular locations will be articulated. I usually ask the participants to write down their thoughts concerning each of the nine major areas of the space, to read these thoughts when we are in those locations, and

OPPOSITE **The Tibetan bowl gong, which is rung by passing the wooden dowel around the outer rim, spirals energy into the heavens. The small cymbals with dragons purify and bless. The period school bell summons our parents. The cast iron bell is decorative.**

The candle symbolizes positive light energy while incense purifys the ceremonial space.

then to place the writings in red envelopes and leave them at the spots as visual reminders. Typical of such thoughts are the wish that a child perform better at school (knowledge/meditation corner), the desire to spend more quality time with the family (family wall), and the hope that a parent's health improves (the mother corner).

When I perform the ceremony, I erect a small altar on a table with various objects that I have brought, which always include at least one representation of each of the four (Western) elements: earth with a rock, fire with a candle, wind with incense, and water with a small cup of water. At the beginning I explain what will happen in the ceremony and then ask the participants to assume the hand position of the heart mudra (palms facing upward, left hand placed on top of right hand, thumbs touching). The ceremony begins with the ringing of Tibetan temple bells. I always perform at least one chant and then reiterate the reasons for the ceremony. We then proceed to each area represented by the ba-gua, where the clients read their statement pertaining to that particular area. One of the most heart felt I remember was a woman's desire to have a child, her first. She was in her thirties, married for the second time, and she fervently wished to start a family before it was too late. At the conclusion of each reading we fold the paper and slip it inside the red envelope, along with rice, to mark the spots where we have been.

The sound of Tibetan temple bells made of seven metals resonates and lingers in the space, marking the beginning and end of the ceremony.

The symbolism within the ceremony is as follows:

The sound of the temple bells is thought to help clear the air of negative aspects and to mark in time the moment the ceremony begins. The piercing quality of the sound is often unexpected and helps focus the attention. The ringing of the bells at the end of the ceremony marks its conclusion, framing the time of the ceremony within.

The heart mudra is symbolic of the lotus, the heart that it represents, and enlightenment. We are, in the West, unaccustomed to postures of devotion (with the exception of kneeling in prayer) or

This blessing mudra, or hand position, symbolizes the lotus.

Objects on this altar represent the harmony of the elements: earth (crystal), wind (incense), fire (candle), water (in the cup), and metal (Tibetan bells).

The carved dragon stamp, called a *chop* in Chinese, engraved with my name, Chin Chien Er (translated as "son of builder, Chin lineage"), is pressed into a red cinnabar paste to consecrate the ceremonial document.

concentration. Symbolic postures increase one's receptivity to spiritual or meditative practices.

The four elements (or five, if the traditional Chinese elements are used) each have their own symbolism, but together they signify the attainment of balance. They are the most basic tools available to the feng shui practitioner to bring harmony, peace, or good fortune to a site and to create a receptive atmosphere for the attainment of the wishes of the client.

The chants are a supplication to God, the natural elements, or the nature within us to align with the purposes of the ceremony and help it to achieve success.

The envelopes contain the thoughts or wishes of the supplicants. This is the most tangible aspect of the ceremony, containing the concrete statements of the clients. Money and rice left in these envelopes are symbolic offerings.

The proper way to pay for a feng shui consultation is with red envelopes that the client should obtain (although they can be provided by the consultant). Sometimes, for added strength for certain cures, multiples of nine are used (such as 9, 18, or 27). Payment for a ceremony, as opposed to a consultation, should *always* be in nine envelopes. Red is a powerful color of high energy and symbolizes an important two-way transfer between the feng shui consultant and the client. If nine envelopes are used it is normal for some of them to contain only token amounts, but there should be *something* in each envelope. If possible, symbolism should be employed in the payment. For instance, one of my clients paid me in nine red envelopes, one of which contained a check; the other eight contained pennies all dated the year that the house had been built. Such a thoughtful payment acknowledges appreciated for the spiritual aspect of the consultation.

Lighting incense in preparation for the blessing ceremony.

I hope that I have given you a deeper understanding of the ancient art of feng shui through these stories. When I discovered feng shui it was a revelation beyond all others. The focus on the individual felt right to me. I found that it has the capacity to help those in need, to bring joy, even comfort to those in pain. The architectural discipline I studied did not have that capacity. But ultimately it was the happiness brought to myself and others through feng shui principles that convinced me that here was an extraordinary gift, an offering that I could, in turn, bring to you.

Let us, then, seek to understand and embrace our surroundings, drawing support from those elements among which we live. Feng shui is the language of space. It is thus a great gift, a blessing, which I now commit to your safekeeping. ∎

CREDITS

All photographs are copyright © 1998 by Francis Hammond except the
   following:
Pages 74, 77–85, 198, 202 (bottom three), 207 (top right) by Keith Trumbo
Pages 196, 203 (top right), 208 (bottom left), 222–223, 224 (top), 225
   by Fred Charles
Page 86 by Anton Wilson
Pages v (bottom), viii–xii, 2–3, 5, 7, 22, 101 are from the author's collection

All drawings and sketches are by the author except as noted:
Page 26: base drawing by Michael McDonough, Architect
Page 62: base drawing by Robert Gaul, Designer
Page 117: base drawing by Frank Lloyd Wright
Page 130: base drawing by Laurie Kerr, Architect
Page 175: base drawing by James Hong, Designer

Credits for supplementary art and furnishings:
Page 213: Bamboo flute and ten emperors' coins–Yun Lin Temple,
   Old Westbury, N.Y.
Pages 24, 28, 106, 202 (top left): 'Money' mirror and 'Relationship'
   mirror: Feng Shui Elements™ designed by R. D. Chin and
   David Rosencrans, New York, N.Y.
Pages 203, 212–213: Noguchi lamps for Akari-Gemini, bamboo screens,
   and red linen Japanese noren–Amie Belobrow of Old Japan,
   New York, N.Y.
Page 203: Desk lamp–IKEA, Elizabeth, N.J.
Page 205: Chinese bamboo birdcage–William Lipton, New York, N.Y.
Pages 204–207: Hand-woven silk fabric backgrounds–Jim Thompson Fabrics,
   New York, N.Y.
Pages 204–205: Ceramics–Sara, New York, N.Y.
Page 204: Red lacquer basket and gilded gourds–Gordon Foster,
   New York, N.Y.
Pages 206, 220: Brass schoolbell, incense and sweetgrass, ceramic bowl,
   and tapestry fabric–Deborah Crowell, New York, N.Y.
Page 190: Soleri bell–Arcosanti, Arizona
Pages 206, 209: Candles, water fountain, and earthenware jug–Fellisimo,
   New York, N.Y.
Pages 182, 188–189, 193: Unique bamboo flutes and vase–Sarajo,
   New York, N.Y.

I N D E X